# Presenting Without Pandering - Self-Marketing for Creatives

Alina Gause

# Presenting Without Pandering - Self-Marketing for Creatives

## A Psychological Guide

Alina Gause
a.way - Counseling for Artists
Berlin
Germany

This book is a translation of the original German edition „Anbieten ohne Anbiedern - Selbstmarketing für Kreative" by Gause, Alina, published by Springer-Verlag GmbH Germany in 2021. The translation was done with the help of artificial intelligence (machine translation by the service DeepL.com). A subsequent human revision was done primarily in terms of content, so that the book will read stylistically differently from a conventional translation. Springer Nature works continuously to further the development of tools for the production of books and on the related technologies to support the authors.

ISBN 978-3-662-64304-4    ISBN 978-3-662-64305-1  (eBook)
https://doi.org/10.1007/978-3-662-64305-1

© Springer-Verlag GmbH Germany, part of Springer Nature 2022

This work is subject to copyright. All rights are reserved by the Publisher, whether the whole or part of the material is concerned, specifically the rights of reprinting, reuse of illustrations, recitation, broadcasting, reproduction on microfilms or in any other physical way, and transmission or information storage and retrieval, electronic adaptation, computer software, or by similar or dissimilar methodology now known or hereafter developed.

The use of general descriptive names, registered names, trademarks, service marks, etc. in this publication does not imply, even in the absence of a specific statement, that such names are exempt from the relevant protective laws and regulations and therefore free for general use.

The publisher, the authors and the editors are safe to assume that the advice and information in this book are believed to be true and accurate at the date of publication. Neither the publisher nor the authors or the editors give a warranty, expressed or implied, with respect to the material contained herein or for any errors or omissions that may have been made. The publisher remains neutral with regard to jurisdictional claims in published maps and institutional affiliations.

This Springer imprint is published by the registered company Springer-Verlag GmbH, DE part of Springer Nature.
The registered company address is: Heidelberger Platz 3, 14197 Berlin, Germany

*"It took me 30 years to become an overnight success."*

Harry Belafonte

# Advance

It does amuse me that I, of all people, am writing a book about self-marketing, as I could well serve as a prime example of an artist who desperately needed such a book to avoid failing so miserably in numerous self-marketing situations, as I have done in the past. Then again, that's exactly why it makes sense for me to write such a book. We know it from all professions: The best teachers and educators are not necessarily those who have gained their skills the easiest way, but those who have a wealth of experience in overcoming hurdles—and I can certainly say that.

The situations in which artists can fail at self-marketing are manifold: photo shoots, castings, self-introductions, conversations in professionally relevant decision-making situations, the selection and production of presentation material, trade fairs, press work, social media, networking meetings, premiere celebrations, award ceremonies, interviews, research, or office work. In addition, the range of withdrawal responses presents itself in all emotional colors: defiance, arrogance, avoidance, anger, depression, projection, envy, numbness, blame, victimhood, fatalism, sarcasm, exhaustion, and more. Creatives have a high (as one would say psychologically) "affective vibratory capacity," which, among many beneficial effects, can also get in the way of one's goals as self-sabotage. This case often occurs when it comes to promoting oneself. So there is absolutely a need for action when it comes to self-marketing, but not all marketing is the same. A book on self-marketing in creative professions must take into account the particularly complicated relationship creative personalities have with the subject. That's why this marketing book is different from others in that it is also a psychological one. I have written it for artists who want to promote themselves successfully and who find a deeper study of themselves and the special laws of the artist's profession and artistic markets helpful in doing so. Those interested in psychological connections and a look behind the scenes will not be disappointed. On the other hand, anyone expecting a "10-steps-to-success plan" will not be happy with this book. The focus is—according to my own biography—on the performing arts, yet the psychological backgrounds are applicable to all creative personalities and genres.

Self-marketing is closely connected to all other aspects of an artist's life. You could say that without self, there is no marketing. Therefore, like building a house, building a marketing strategy should be done from the foundation and not from the chimney. For this reason, the first part of this book deals with your personal attitude towards self-marketing and associated resistance. You will develop a basic attitude that will make you your own "partner in crime." In the second part, we turn to the selection and preparation of concrete activities and launch initial ventures. The main focus is on finding a mode of action that you can sustain for long enough. Finally, in the third part, we arrive at concrete tips and practical exercises such as preparing photo sessions, designing a profile in social networks, or negotiating contracts—topics that others already expect at the beginning of a book on self-marketing. You may have come a long way by then, but you hold in your hand insights that go beyond the realm of self-marketing and can advance your artistic and personal life just as much.

I have been advising creatives of all genres since 2009. I initially started with a hypothesis of what support in this profession should look like, which had developed from my artistic CV and my knowledge as a psychologist. Today, this hypothesis has become a convinced attitude: There are clear rules and strategies for personal success. Deal with them and you can lead a life that satisfies you privately, artistically, and existentially.

Self-marketing—presenting yourself and your art to the world—can be fun. And fun is the only fuel that convinces creative personalities. Not in the sense of brief thrills or light entertainment, but in the sense of fulfillment, visionary meaningfulness, and flow experience. I want to promise nothing less than that to those who follow me through this book.

Berlin, Germany  Alina Gause
February 2020

# Acknowledgment

I would like to thank Springer Verlag for the renewed trust and support. To Monika Mühlhausen for the project management, Shahbaz Alam for accompanying the production process, and especially to Joachim Coch for the editing, the detailed answers to my many questions, his fine intuition, and the always appreciative attitude. Thank you, Nikita Dhiwar, for supervising the creation process of the English version.

I would also like to thank Karoline Klemke and Heike Scharpff for their expertise and attention to detail in the reading of the manuscript and their helpful suggestions. Thank you for your time!

Thank you, Jack Lord, for working with me on the English translation—it has been an inspiring and wonderful time!

Furthermore, my special thanks go to Anna Piro-Lauble. I am very happy that her wonderfully creative and lively illustrations have become a part of this book.

Thank you Andreas, for always managing, as a first-time reader of everything I write, to convince me to venture outside with it.

As in every one of my non-fiction books about creatives, I would like to conclude by thanking the many exciting personalities who have placed their trust in me over the years and told me about their longings, worries, and hardships. The moments when they wanted to sink into the ground with shame and those brimming with fulfillment and devotion with what they experienced with their art. I wish them all to be seen and heard.

# Contents

**Introduction**........................................... 1
In the First Step We Turn to Your Inner Attitude .......... 9
With the Right Posture at Your Back, the Second Step Is
  to Get into Action ................................. 9
Finally, Step 3 Deals with Being Visible ................ 10

## Part I  Find the Right Posture

**The Early Stage: Your Reliable Engine** ............... 19
References........................................ 32

**Where Is My Habitat?: No More "How Do I Have
to Be?"** .............................................. 33

**Shame: No Artistic Flourishing Without Dignity**........ 39
References........................................ 53

**Overcoming the "Ouch Complex": Feeling Good Is a
Must** ................................................. 55

**Help Is at Hand: Discover Your *Third Person*** .......... 61

## Part II  Get into Action

**The Vicious Circle of Self-Marketing: Why Too Much Market Blocks Creativity** ............................ 77

**The Angelic Ladder of Self-Marketing: Caring for the Creative Core Is the Key** ............................ 85

**The Quarter-Hour Policy: Finding Space and Time** ..... 97

**Office Time: Your Essential Tool for Climbing the Mountain** ............................................. 103

**The Work Wish List: Networking According to Your Taste** ................................................ 107

## Part III  Be Visible

**Life in Business: Who's Who and Who Does What, and Why You Should Know** ........................... 115

**Excursus: Not Me!—What #metoo Has to Do with Self-Marketing** ............................................ 119

**The Right Support: Coaches, Agents and More** ......... 135

**Excursus 2: Negotiations** ............................ 149

**Presentation Material: Photos, Website, Social Networks Et al.** ....................................... 155
Photos ................................................ 155

**In Conclusion** ...................................... 171

**References** ......................................... 173

# Introduction

What I write down on the subject of self-marketing mirrors the encounters and development processes I have experienced in the course of my work as an artist, lecturer, consultant and manager. This gives a good insight into the current living and working conditions in the creative industry, which are directly related to what kind of marketing makes sense. A lot has happened since 1985, when I entered the art business professionally. On the one hand, a lot of good things have happened: #metoo has brought us intimacy coaches on film sets. Musical singers in many places are compensated as they are in the opera genre because it's understood that the vocal stakes are comparable. At some theaters, evening rehearsals are waived once in a while if the team is well on schedule. There is the possibility of carrying out risk assessments of mental stress, tailored to the needs of artistic professions (as has long been the practice for other professions). Institutes specialising in medical care for dancers and musicians that provide profession-specific support. The Internet offers artists a variety of platforms to build up a fan base or sell their products without the need for distribution groups. The first art fairs are exhibiting artists without the mediation of a gallery. On the other hand, many things are still as they always were: the cliché of the "crazy artist" who is the only one who can be a "true artist" is still widespread in many places. The same applies to the stigma that gainful employment outside the artistic field automatically degrades artists. Theatres are producing more premieres than ever before, but this is not reflected in the fees of those working in the arts. Artists can hardly live on their income and are threatened by poverty in old age. Some orchestra musicians know no other way to help themselves than to get a grip on their stage fright with beta-blockers or other drugs sold under the counter. Many negative consequences of stress—such as exhaustion, injuries or instability—are still too often regarded as necessary side effects of an artist's life and are therefore not prevented. When I recently taught the graduating class at a German performing arts college, I was shocked: these exhausted and discouraged talents were supposed to launch into a life of peak performance in the next few weeks? I like to compare the artistic profession with high-performance sports. There is no question that for elite athletes to achieve maximum results a dedicated team with unique skill sets must be put in place. Not from any philanthropic standpoint, but because this optimizes performance, which in turn optimizes success. Creatives need to be, or assemble, their own team. This requires self-care and strategic thinking, which I would like to encourage with this book.

For the team idea, I have developed the concept of "The Three Personality Parts of Creative People", which I would now like to introduce you to directly: As a creative personality, you already have a personal core team consisting of the first personality part, your private self, the second personality part, your artist self and the third personality part, which I call the *Third Person*. This *Third Person* appears in situations that are not clearly private or artistic, and these include all around self-marketing without exception. Here one thinks classically first of professional presentations or applications. But also, for example, at the moment when your table neighbour at a private birthday party turns out to be an attractive employer for you, the first person—your private person—says goodbye and the *Third Person* appears. Or else at the rehearsal: you are acting, i.e. your second person—the creative one—is active. There is an interruption and the director, the lecturer, the conductor, the choreographer or a colleague addresses you: at this moment you step out of your artist ego and the *Third Person* is called upon. The distinction between these three personality parts is important for many reasons, which I will discuss in detail later in the book. One, however, should be mentioned now: Each of these personality parts activates different states of consciousness and levels of competency. It is of considerable importance for your success that you know about the strengths and weaknesses of your three personalities and that you can switch from one to the other without great irritation.

Every now and then I am asked what exactly the *Third Person* can be translated as. Person 1 = private self. Person 2 = creative ego. And the *Third Person*? I don't want to call it anything other than simply: the *Third Person*. Part of the exercise will be to associate your own personal inner designation with it. A client with whom I exchanged ideas about a substantive title for her *Third Person* wrote to me: *"For me personally, I called it my "manager ego" and imagined it as an egg-laying jack-in-the-box, a mixture of caring mommy and well-negotiating businesswoman."*

Many creatives identify the *Third Person* as their biggest construction site. They experience them as helpless, incompetent and powerless. Referring to the example of the birthday party, the moment the person sitting next to them reveals themselves to be a successful director, film or music producer, they seem to lose access to everything that person one and two otherwise have at their disposal for winning communication: charm, humour, acumen, persuasiveness, knowledge, enthusiasm or passion. It's understandable why the *Third Person* is often the weakling of the trio: creatives don't usually become artists and performers because they love to sell. And so, while the *Third Person* is responsible for marketing, it rarely lives up to its important role because it is often left out in the cold, unprepared and unloved. If you don't provide your *Third Person* with the necessary know-how, it will take revenge by making you disappear from the market and, to make matters worse, will shower you with accusations and complaints:

> "Why am *I* not up there now?"
> "I wish you had done this five years ago!"
> "It's all just a drop in the ocean."
> "Life is unfair."
> "Wow - that was embarrassing!"

With this book I want to change that for you. There is a huge discrepancy within the *Third Person*: the importance of navigating the market on the one hand and the insufficient training and equipment for this important task on the other. For this reason I have dedicated a whole book to this personality part and the topic of self-marketing.

> Not if or what, but how and now!

When someone first hears me speak—in a workshop, at a lecture, or in one-on-one counseling—on the topic of self-marketing, I know I have a crucial hurdle to clear, as summed up by one singer after our first meeting: "*I thought I was walking out of here with an Instagram guide.*" I have to disappoint expectations like that. I know how much creatives in particular wish all you had to do was get your hands on the right tools and self-marketing would turn out to be a breeze. I take a different approach. This is not by chance, but comes from knowledge from over 10 years of consulting and management of creative people, also my background knowledge as a psychologist and last but not least my personal experience from 30 years of artistic work. From these influences arose the desire to offer artists something that would have convinced me myself. No simple solutions for complicated issues, but a holistic and sustainable understanding—as a human being and creative personality. I make no secret of the fact that I reject simplistic approaches based on a lack of knowledge of psychological processes, creative personalities and work, because they are grist to the mill of harmful clichés and prevent an appropriate appreciation of artists. No profession is simultaneously so despised and so exalted. On the one hand, they are more or less lovingly ridiculed as cranks who devote their lives to dubious self-fulfillment that is utterly useless to the world and therefore not necessarily worthy of adequate pay. On the other hand, they can be adored, envied and favoured beyond measure (and claim horrendous fees accordingly). George Clooney's mother is reported to have once said to him: "*You were never as bad as they wrote and you were never as good as they wrote.*" A more adequate appreciation of what creative professions are and accomplish would enable them to value their contribution more highly and use it more consciously themselves as well. In times of globalisation, individualisation, changing gender roles or digitalisation, we are all confronted with societal changes that artists have always had to deal with in their lives, and so they have experience of dealing with them ahead of many people. Almost every job requirement profile today contains the word "creativity". And this despite the fact that no one knows exactly what is meant by it. What constitutes creativity? What are the prerequisites for it? How much is it worth to us to achieve it? If we want to learn more about it, we have to take a serious look at creative personalities and processes. This is as true for people who have no connection to the artistic profession as it is for you. And so back to the topic at hand.

Nothing would be easier than to share an Instagram tutorial. You could even standardize that: "copy and paste"—in 5 min the thing would be done.

> "10 Steps to Successful Self-Marketing!"
> "Social Media - Become a Star in Three Months!"
> "All the Tricks of the Trait to Breakthrough at a Glance!".

I think that's either ignorant or unprofessional. Handing creatives something like that would feel like giving them a cake recipe but shrugging it off when they ask, "I don't have any electricity—now what?" and replying, "That's not my problem. I've told you everything you need to know." From my perspective, however, the issue for artists when it comes to marketing themselves is entirely about electricity. Not about *if* it needs to be done—hardly anyone doubts that self-marketing is part of the job. Nor about *what* needs to be done—for the most part creatives know this because they follow closely what others are doing. There is little need for action here, but the widest range of advice, books, workshops or complementary study events. However, if you start exclusively here—on the "if or what"—it can have the opposite of the intended effect, even with useful content. Some nod dutifully while thinking "It's too late. You can't make up for what you've missed so far. You're not suited for this job. Everyone else can do better." They go home and block out the notes from the lecture or the underlined passages in the book like a bad exam result. Others may be highly motivated, "Yes—I feel that today and here I am in the right frame of mind to become top-notch at self-marketing!" It's not uncommon for this momentum to only last anywhere from a minute to a few weeks, followed by a plunge into a crisis of purpose and self-esteem. You may be wondering how I can be so confident in the scenarios whilst they seem so full of drama to you? If so, I suspect you are a relative, friend or partner but do not practice a creative profession yourself?

> What I write down is based on the observation of situations and courses in the biographies of creative people whom I have followed or accompanied for over 30 years.

The answer is, I'm never sure but it's always dramatic. This has to do with the existential significance of artistic activity for the identity of a creative personality. The product to be marketed is closely connected to the body, mind and soul of the person selling it. Therefore it can be destructive if it turns out to be hardly saleable and psychologically draining when showcasing feels like striptease. Likewise when the creative process develops a momentum of its own that runs counter to market requirements.

People who have a high degree of creativity approach projects differently than others. This also applies to the project marketing. This should be taken into account by, on the one hand, using the helpful aspects of this difference and, on the other hand, not jeopardizing the flow by using the less useful ones. What creatives often lack is the psychological know-how to motivate themselves, or at least not sabotage themselves, to get their art out there. The question they need an answer to is: How do I have to design my self-marketing so that I can apply it continuously and thus sustainably?

> So the main question is not *if* self-marketing is useful or *what* the right tools are but *how* to make it suit your personality and thus guarantee that it can actually happen *now*.

This book is intended to contribute to this. The basis for this is provided by the following five principles, the practical implementation of which we will address in the course of reading:

1. **Take a look behind the scenes!**
   It is crucial that you are clear about the background of what you are doing or not doing.
2. **Think long term!**
   The first thing is to get into action, but then also to stay in action, and that over decades.
3. **Take yourself with you!**
   Design your approach to this in such a way that it causes as little friction with your personality as possible. Otherwise it cannot be done, and therefore, in most cases, it will not be done.
4. **Think strategically!**
   What is the product you want to offer? Where do you want to go with it? What is the effort/return ratio of your self-marketing that you are aiming for?
5. **Keep form and content flexible!**
   Always adapt your approach to new life circumstances, changing goals or balance sheets.

## In the First Step We Turn to Your Inner Attitude

Certainly, the attitude with which a person approaches something is important for everyone, but with creative personalities the difference is striking. If they find access to their creative source, it's like turning them on; conversely, if they can't connect with themselves or have to act against an inner conviction, it's like pulling the plug. Promoting yourself or your art can be an ordeal that makes life hell. But it can also be a natural process that is also fun. Attitude is the first step towards turning the former into the latter. Such an attitude cannot be developed overnight—moreover, if it is foreign to you. It has to be worked out on the mental level and then applied concretely. Only as a result of this will feelings change.

## With the Right Posture at Your Back, the Second Step Is to Get into Action

The effect of simply doing something is still underestimated. Or as the actor Götz George liked to say: "*Don't talk. Do.*" Self-marketing can be so exhausting and annoying for creative personalities that I recommend not investing 1 min of your life, not one cent of your already meager income, and not one spark of your creative energy in a direction that doesn't match your own. Instead, go directly to the market segment that fits your product with the resources that fit your personality.

# Finally, Step 3 Deals with Being Visible

If the attitude is right and you have come into action, you will automatically become visible. Now you could say: goal achieved—this is where the book ends. But for some, this is where the problem begins. For many artists, the fact that self-marketing means that you have to leave your own shelter and become visible in order to reach your goal is the real hurdle. Therefore, the third step that this book will be about is that of dealing with being visible. If one is in agreement with being in the limelight, it is ensured that the approach will also last in the long term.

The secret to successful self-marketing is when you feel welcome where you show up. Then the ordeal is over and it starts to be fun: Presenting without pandering. To do that, you have to discover yourself, and show yourself.

# Part I

## Find the Right Posture

A self-care, strategic, long-term mindset takes some getting used to for many artists. There are three reasons for this: first, they can better identify with acting spontaneously and from a feeling. Secondly, their above-average commitment and capacity for suffering sometimes makes them lose sight of the big picture here. Thirdly, before and during their training, it was all about their artistic abilities, and this tended to follow the passive mode of "being discovered". The parents, artistic mentors discover the talent, the selection process of the training institution continues the principle. One sings, plays, paints, invents, dances and from outside someone watches and says: "You! We'll choose you and give you special attention and encouragement." If someone doesn't bother promoting themselves until they graduate, the wheel still doesn't stop turning. However, that changes when you graduate. Sometimes there's still a transitional period where you're a newcomer, placed through the recommendation of a mentor at the university or training school (and charging less than those who are already established). Not long after that, it becomes noticeable: if you follow the principle of being discovered, you won't work much. Unfortunately, young talent is sometimes led to believe that it is effective:

## Find the Right Posture

> "I saw him and felt right away that he had that certain something."
> "I happened to get hold of her demo and immediately called the management."
> "She just wanted to accompany her friend to the audition - she ended up getting the part."
> "He uploaded it to YouTube and then it went viral!"

Stories like these are told and disseminated through the media because we love stories. Artists love stories more than anyone else and are therefore particularly receptive to them. It also fits with the longing to be discovered. However, once you've experienced the invention of supposedly personal stories as part of a PR strategy, you lose your innocent faith in the unconditional authenticity of it. I know of cases where the people concerned had a hard time freeing themselves from the web of falsehoods and half-truths later on.

> I want to call on creatives to tell their own story and use it in a self-determined way for their marketing.

So for you, the right attitude for successful self-marketing is first of all to check whether you are (still) following the passive mode, and then get ready to change it into an active mode by reading this book.

There are an infinite number of reasons not to take on the topic of self-marketing, and at least as many to do it anyway. Unfortunately, the reasons that keep us from doing it are often more profound and therefore more actionable than those that motivate us. I sometimes work with the concept of the Hero's Journey (Campbell 1994; Vogler 1998), which I'm sure is well known to the screenwriters

## Find the Right Posture

among you. The hero's journey describes a scheme that underlies most stories and can be described in abbreviated form like this: The hero/heroine, answering a call, sets out from the known world to conquer an unknown one. After overcoming an initial inner resistance, he or she, encouraged by mentors, takes on the battle with monsters and other trials in order to finally obtain the elixir, which must then survive the return journey home unharmed. In the end, what has been gained is united with the old and thus "the master of two worlds" is created (see illustration "Hero's Journey"). When an artist sets out to tackle the unloved subject of self-marketing, it is comparable to such an adventure journey. The "call of the market" manifests itself either in the form of general or artistic dissatisfaction, unsatisfied ambition or disappointed demands, lack of commissions or the simple realization of the need for increased self-marketing in order to become more visible. This is usually followed by some avoidance and resistance circles:

> "First I'll rehearse/practice/workout/phone/gamble/eat/watch a show, then I'll tackle it …"
> "Only those who are bad have the need to advertise themselves so overtly."
> "I'm just not cut out for this."

Finally, various mentors cross the path of the travelers—partners, lecturers, coaches, colleagues, friends, family. Sometimes I am the first to try to get them to present themselves better. According to the concept of the Hero's Journey, we are then facing the "first threshold" and thus the "path of trials". This is a delicate moment, because right in front of us is the unpleasant part. So, my job is to present this part realistically on the one hand, but also to keep my counterpart from taking flight on the other. Sometimes I then skip that part first and ask, "What should be in the pot at the end? What's your elixir?". So, when I hear from an actor, for example, "I'd like to shoot a little more.", or from a theater director, "Next year, get offered something different than the Christmas fairy tale.". From an opera singer: "Do a concert once in a while in addition to my house commitments.". From a singer-songwriter: "Get my name out there a bit.". Additionally: design a new website, establish a higher fee level, understand social media, create new photos, maybe seek an agency change. Then I know he or she isn't yet in the frame of mind to expose themselves to the dangers and struggles of the "path of trials." Don't get me wrong: there's nothing wrong with a new website and higher fees, or wanting to get your name out there a bit, but these are just first steps. First "trials" on the way to the real "elixir". Taken on their own, these goals will hardly be able to take on the monsters—at the first hurdle (e.g. negative feedback or a bad investment), the reverse is true.

The prospect of the harvest must be strong enough to stand against the moments of shame, fear, confrontation with one's own limitations and weaknesses that lurk along the way. Otherwise, the need to retreat to a safe haven—the "known world"—will win out. Therefore, before answering the "call", I think it is important to first think carefully about what the real goal of the journey is.

The distinction between values and goals from *Acceptance and Commitment Therapy* (ACT) can be helpful here (Harris 2009, 2013). Values are comparable to guiding principles that can guide and motivate us as we move through life; goals, on the other hand, are to be seen as important intermediate stations that we can aim for and achieve along the way. Accordingly, it is possible to check off goals while values remain with us in the process of life. Russ Harris gives a vivid example of this (taken from his work materials): *"No matter how far west you go, you never reach "the west"!"*. So, in order to be able to set intermediate goals and not shy away from realizing them, we want to make sure that you are in alignment with your personal value system—your greatest source of strength:

> What is the deep meaning of being visible for you, of exchange, of being seen and heard, for which it is worth enduring a lot?
> What is your "elixir" in this story?
> What happens when you hold it in your hands - how do you integrate the new with the old?
> Will partners, the ensemble, circle of friends, colleagues be unanimously happy for you when you reinvent yourself, appear in full size and celebrate success?

**Find the Right Posture**

**The Hero's Journey**

In the following, we'll look at the most common psychological hurdles that hinder creative heroes and heroines in self-marketing on their "path of trials," and I'll suggest ways of thinking about and practicing how to overcome them:

- *Hurdle 1: Lack of drive*
- "The Early Stage—Your reliable engine".
- *Hurdle 2: Wrong environments*
- "Where is my Habitat?"—No more "How do I have to be?"
- *Hurdle 3: Shame*
- "Shame—No artistic flourishing without dignity".
- *Hurdle 4: A hard look at yourself*
- "Overcoming the "Ouch Complex"—Feeling good is a must."
- *Hurdle 5: Structure*
- "Help is at Hand—Discover your *Third Person*".

# References

Campbell, Joseph (1994). *Die Kraft der Mythen. Bilder der Seele im Leben des Menschen.* Zürich: Artemis & Winkler.

Harris, Russ (2013). *Wer vor dem Schmerz flieht, wird von ihm eingeholt: Unterstützung in schwierigen Zeiten. ACT in der Praxis.* München: Kösel-Verlag.

Harris, Russ (2009). *Wer dem Glück hinterherrennt, läuft daran vorbei: Ein Umdenkbuch.* München: Kösel.

Vogler, Christopher (1998). *Die Odyssee des Drehbuchschreibers.* 2., aktualisierte und erweiterte Auflage. Frankfurt am Main: Zweitausendeins.

# The Early Stage: Your Reliable Engine

Your attitude towards offering yourself and your art is crucial to the success of everything you plan to do, so it's important to clarify what your fundamental drive is in life as a first step. I said at the beginning that for creatives, self-marketing is all about power, i.e. how to make sure you keep at it. There are many different models and concepts to explain or strengthen a person's motivation. Some more evolutionary biology-oriented approaches see us as close to animals in basic features and therefore our behavior is primarily focused on defending territories, food sources or spreading our genes. That being said, there are psychological models, many of which are based on Abraham Maslow's pyramid of needs, which I will discuss at the end of this chapter. My own preference in working with creatives is for concepts with emotionally meaningful content and language rich in imagery. Approaches that evoke a phase of life that was characterized by free play, unadulterated expression and curiosity, and thus usually associated with the birth of your second person—the artist ego. So, it is not by chance that I started with the "Hero's Journey" and would like to introduce you to the concept of the "Early Stage" in the following.

To do this, we go back to the time when you had your first encounters with the public and gathered your first insights into what reactions you trigger in your environment with your actions. In which you made your first performances like words, steps and facial expressions. Followed by Lego towers, songs, dances and pictures. In which you made your first decisions and mistakes. Our evaluation of what we accomplish is decisively influenced by the evaluations of our environment during this time. We orient ourselves by the reactions, looks and statements or the absence of the same. This also applies to our assessment of pain or danger. We look into the face of our closest caregiver to be able to classify our perception. If she remains relaxed, we may also relax. If she sees a reason to cheer in our performance, we are proud. If her brow is furrowed, we doubt. In this phase, i.e. already in the first years of life, basic motivations are formed, which remain with us throughout our lives. Bit by bit, a deep conviction is formed about which goals we consider worth striving for and how we assess our means to achieve them (if you want to know more about this, research the terms "social referencing" and "self-efficacy"). This attitude is so profound that it can still show up 30 years later when we have a hard time writing to a theater, drafting a post for Instagram, or writing a press release, even though from the outside it seems child's play. We internalized at a much earlier stage how the world we live in works. That may not be the same as what we were taught in that workshop, book or seminar on marketing. Our deep-seated self refuses to be tricked by our current self, which thinks self-marketing is a great thing. Instead, we stick to the principle that has been established over decades.

> Developing a constructive attitude towards self-marketing therefore needs good arguments, continuous input, patience and above all self-love.

It leads nowhere to work against the proven value system. It is more effective to use the already established one. For this I like to fall back on the concept of the "Early Stage", as Irmtraud Tarr Krüger (1993) calls these learned connections. We enter the "Early Stage" in the early years of our lives, laying the foundation for our beliefs about what is worth striving for. We develop our preferred "elixir." After that, there are four aspects that drive us humans individually:

1. Love
2. Power
3. Meaning
4. Victory

Each of these aspects has a certain attractiveness for each of us, but usually one or two appeal to us strongly and one or two less. Check for yourself in the following statements which of the four aspects appeals to you more or less emotionally. Three preliminary remarks:

1. Try to refrain from judging the terms. They are words that automatically invoke positive or negative connotations through their linguistic use. In this context, however, they are to be considered value-free. None of the aspects is morally superior or inferior to the other.
2. In all aspects, the drive within us arises equally from striving for the positive pole as from rejecting the negative pole.
3. The aim is to identify the most efficient fuel for you personally.

**Love**
(or the avoidance of being unloved)

Here the focus is on the connection to other people. Resonance and exchange are sought. One likes to reassure oneself that one is not alone, that one is understood, recognized, noticed and liked. Conversely, one also likes to invest in avoiding the opposite. The drive comes from the desire to fulfill the basic need for harmony and security.

> **Example Erich, Composer and Pianist**
>
> Due to the fact that Erich spent his childhood with a depressive mother and an absent father, he had to manage almost entirely without resonance in all formative phases. Whatever he did—he was hardly noticed and rarely given recognition. A brief digression on this: There is a psychological research video that has stuck in my mind powerfully. It shows a mother suffering from depression with her 6-month-old infant. The infant tries with all means to get in contact with his mother. He gurgles, laughs, squeals, kicks his legs and gesticulates wildly—the mother looks at him and no movement can be read from her face. We watch as this infant is emotionally starved—it is devastating. The instruction had been, "Please play and communicate with your child as you do at home." After about 10 min, the experimenter repeats the instruction, assuming the mother had not understood it before. But the mother replies, "I know. That's exactly what I did." How dramatic that must have been for the mother herself and subsequently for this expectant human being! Erich must have experienced something similar. Our work could not be about healing this old pain. But we understood that resonance, recognition, connection—in a word, love—was for him the highest good to strive for. An elixir for which he was more than willing to take on some dragons. He put his insight into practice by asking the audience to perform a communal act at the beginning of every concert from then on (so as not to reveal his identity, I cannot say in detail what that act was). In this way he did not perceive the audience as an anonymous mass in the dark, but established a connection with them. In future, he also attached great importance to entering into conversation with the individual musicians in the run-up to the rehearsal of his compositions—about similarities in biography or the view of the work.

> **Example Irene, Cellist**
>
> Irene came from a large and very successful family of musicians. As is sometimes the case in musical families, the instruments are not necessarily distributed first and foremost according to preferences, but rather according to what is conducive to home music. Irene completed a family string quartet with the cello. Her talent was far above average and she was also extremely hard-working, so many doors opened for her to pursue a promising career. But for Irene this did not turn out to be a blessing: She suffered from severe stage fright, and there were also pains while playing. Nevertheless, she continued to make music undeterred—she won competition after competition and eventually received invitations to audition for renowned ensembles. It took her many years of her life to find out that an opportunity that would have been the greatest dream for most musicians and also for many of her family members, meant for her to give up the most important thing: Connectedness. A solo career in the classical music market fulfils many desires—the one for a steady social life and building a family of one's own is not necessarily one of them. Musicians know this and find their own best compromise for all the conflicting goals. Irene first had to almost completely lose her desire for life—to get up in the morning and look forward to what was to come—before she could accept that the drive of her parents, siblings, cousins was not her own. She studied music for a teaching degree and now lives with her husband and children not far from her childhood home in a medium-sized city. She no longer has any problems with the drive or pain when playing.

**Power**

(or the avoidance of feeling powerless)

The term power refers to the desire to take the lead, to make decisions, to hold the reins of one's own destiny in one's hands. Freedom is in the foreground as a basic need. To be able to shape things oneself sets the motor in motion. The idea, on the other hand, of not being able to influence one's own destiny, of being dependent on others and powerless in important life conditions, stifles one's own initiative.

> **Example Beate, Actor and Screenwriter**
>
> Beate sought me out to improve her employment situation as an actor. We developed a strategy on how she could renew her material and apply for stage and film. I often ask my clients to give me feedback after 2 weeks on whether the theoretical plan is working in practice. She reported that she was not succeeding in motivating herself to take the steps we thought would be useful. So, we checked whether the expected effort and hoped-for return were in good proportion. Actors are exposed to a high degree of powerlessness, often surrendering control resulting in a lack of influence. This applies both to the part of their professional life in which they seek engagement and to the work itself. Of course, roles differ in this as well, but those whose main drive is to have all decisions in their own hands are more likely to be unhappy in this profession. Those who are happy to surrender and trust in leadership will have fewer inner conflicts to overcome. For Beate, it turned out that being able to decide freely about herself was a deep concern. How much do I work? When and where? On what? With whom? Can I bring in my own artistic ideas? Will I achieve my goal with my own initiative? The immense effort it would have meant for her to reposition herself on the acting market would not have brought her what she longed for in the end. And so, consequently, she didn't. Today she is a screenwriter. This profession also holds many challenges, but she faces them with a different energy. The market is more transparent and with a high degree of initiative, she has managed to establish herself in a film genre that she particularly enjoys. She decides for herself how many assignments she will accept in a year. She is free to choose her co-authors, determines her own working hours and locations, and realizes her own ideas.

> **Example Theo, Actor**
>
> Theo counters the fact that powerlessness is part of his profession, but that he as a person likes to be in charge, by being involved in professional politics. He has always taken on tasks for the whole ensemble more often than others, and found that this did not seem unfair to him, but—on the contrary—increased his general motivation to work. When we identified power as his preferred basic drive, he consciously increased his commitment and ultimately took on a leadership position in a theatre, which he still enjoys doing years later.

## Meaning

(or the avoidance of meaninglessness)

Here, the basic human need for self-realization is in the foreground. Content and sustainability as well as the uniqueness of one's own contribution are important. If the desired goal is subjectively felt to be of importance in the world, the drive to achieve it seems inexhaustible. Conversely Insignificance—symbolized, for example, by being replaceable and ephemeral—removes motivation.

> **Example Simon, Singer and Actor**
>
> For a singer and actor with dance training, at first glance the musical business offers itself as a field of work. So, Simon was also working in this market at the time of our collaboration. A musical performer has to develop a good audition repertoire and continuously apply for auditions with it. Simon no longer understood the world: He, who was actually able to work in a disciplined and goal-oriented manner, sabotaged himself by preparing too late and inadequately. This meant that his chances of finding work were close to zero. He wanted to change that, he told me. We talked at length about the musical business, what he liked about it and what he didn't. It turned out that it was mostly the interchangeability that bothered him. Why embark on a he-

ro's journey, train every day like a high-performance athlete, subject himself to the constant selection process, when the elixir at the end is the *"11th cast change in a stage entertainment production, where it doesn't matter who plays it as long as the notes and steps and phrases are acted out as given?"*. It happens quickly that one's own subjective assessment is confused with an objective universal assessment. Because for others, "being the 11th cast change in a stage entertainment production" is the fulfillment of all dreams. For him, it wasn't. He identified meaning as his first basic drive and we built all marketing efforts on that: The photos no longer showed him as "Everybody's Darling" but as a character head, he chose the auditions very carefully—those that were of significance to him in terms of content, he prepared intensively. Today, he is still active in musicals, though he has made a name for himself for character roles and challenging vocal parts. Knowing that this orientation also held existential risks for him (because he only wanted to do what covered his basic drive), he looked for another field of activity that would secure him financially in times of crisis.

### Example Rea, Dancer

Rea reported that she was increasingly lacking passion for her profession. We looked at her daily work and found that the highlights were to be found where she was challenged in a special way, such as when she had to take over a difficult solo from a colleague who had fallen ill within a very short time. Or when there was a technical or other breakdown during a performance and it was of high importance whether she could solve this problem well. Or when she was asked for her opinion in the design process. When she identified meaning as the strongest basic drive for her, it changed her view of the ways in which she had to be involved in the theatre business in order to feel her own personal contribution. Today she is studying alongside her work as a dancer in order to be able to express her own personal signature as a choreographer in the future.

> **Example Aline, Performer**
>
> *For years I thought I wanted to be loved so badly. Maybe because that's what we perfomers are always told. It's not true at all. I actually don't care if they love me when I step in front of an audience with a role. It's much more important to me that they remember me afterwards. It totally relieves me to know that it's the content and my own personal contribution that drives me. I relate to that a lot more.*

## Victory

(or the avoidance of defeat)

A clear goal—first place, not second—and a direct path to it make the heart beat faster and mobilize forces. These energies can be released just as much to escape an impending defeat. Victory as the strongest source of drive is to be understood as a sporting spirit that is not directed against others, but on the contrary needs interesting opponents to guarantee an exciting competition.

> **Example: Dörthe, Director**
>
> In her case, looking at the likes and clicks on Instagram was a welcome competition: *"This month I want to break the 100,000 barrier."* What is an agonizing challenge for a person for whom the meaning of their actions is paramount, because it seems fast-moving and devoid of content, was easy for her to accomplish and sweetened her everyday life as a game with a competitive character.

> **Example: Hanna, Freelance Writer**
>
> Hanna worked for a lifestyle magazine and came to me because she wanted to improve her presentations. She already lacked verve in the run-up to the presentation and thus dragged out the preparation. Then she was blocked and

> scared when she had to present her ideas to the team. We realized that she was looking for motivation in the wrong place: In the content of the magazine, whose target audience was teenagers. She expected herself to draw from her identification with the content the drive to prepare enthusiastically and to command attention in team meetings. As a first step, she had to acknowledge that she was deeply bored with the content. For a person whose main drive is the meaningfulness of what they do, this would have been an insurmountable obstacle. Not for Hanna, for she named victory as her favored drive. As a result, we looked for where there was something to gain within her work and found it in market share. Hanna could get very excited about having captured the highest market share at the end of a quarter. When she talked about how the shares had evolved, there was no longer a need to laboriously struggle to improve her rhetoric and vocal presence—she felt in her element. Henceforth, she consciously sought out opportunities to combine her desire to compete with her professional activities. And with this changed basic attitude, she found it easier to present her ideas and also to assert herself in a team. Ultimately, it led to her leaving the magazine for another, international medium where she was surrounded by kindred sparring partners.

The case studies show that it is not helpful to devalue ourselves or others for the way we or they are structured. Devaluations of this kind only lead us to chase after the image of a personality that we consider to be more socially compatible, morally superior or more promising than our true self. And then wonder why life is so hard. Going against your own nature takes a lot of energy. No one alignment of character is better than another. Rather, the goal should be to know yourself well enough to live as much as possible in alignment with your own interests and values. In the end, this is how we deal with contented people. Satisfied people are usually more efficient, more generous, more tolerant, healthier and more peaceful.

Take the first step in marketing yourself by taking a moment to identify your basic drive:

> **Exercise Basic Drive**
>
> Imagine different scenarios for each of the aspects in which you have or must give up love, power, meaning, or victory.
> Can you notice any differences in the intensity of your reaction to the imagined situation?
> Rank the four aspects for yourself.
> Take these preliminary findings into your everyday life and see if your impression is confirmed.
> Can you sustainably identify one or two basic drives as your preferred ones?
> What can be used to satisfy these needs?

As already mentioned, there are other motivational models besides the "Early Stage" way of thinking to get to the bottom of the origin of your engine. I would like to conclude by referring to Abraham Maslow's well-known Hierarchy of Needs (Maslow 1943), which names five basic human needs:

1. Physiological needs,
2. Safety,
3. Love/Belonging,
4. Self-Esteem and
5. Self-Actualization.

Artistic professions are mainly in areas 4 and 5—creative people mainly follow the need for free, individual expression and self-realization. It is not uncommon for basic physiological needs, the need for security and social relationships to be pushed into the background. The concept of the first, second and *Third Person* takes this into account and reminds you that, in addition to the artist self, you also remain a human being who needs to be cared for. After all, priorities, and therefore available sources of strength, can change quickly when we find ourselves in crisis. For example, during the Corona crisis I received many letters like the one below from Imogen, who laments that she lacks the drive to market herself.

It should be noted that all the questions from artists printed in this book and my answers to them have already appeared once in "ca:stmag". With my column, the actors' magazine has been offering its readers an anonymous platform for their personal, profession-specific questions since 2008.

### Imogen, 37

*I'm writing to you as a push for myself, so to speak, to get myself out of this slump. I'm sure I don't have to explain to you what the acting world is like right now. Like everyone, I first relaxed, then whined, and now I'm ready to put myself back together. Of course, the question of meaning lurks in the background, because now even those who were completely carefree before Corona have nothing to do. Do you have any nudge for me on how to find the strength to care about my job in all of this?*

### Alina Gause

The bad news is that the to-do list for artists has not changed as a result of the crisis: You're supposed to remember those who could cast you, update your material and produce new material if necessary, maintain and expand your network. I realize that this message is unlikely to get your engine started. But there is also a good message that is more helpful: The pressure of suffering in crisis causes us to look more deeply at our own path. For example, how we can recharge our batteries. And what the meaning of it all is. In order to approach the answer to this question, we have to think beyond shooting days, castings, showreels and agencies. Performers don't usually start out on their path to become rich and famous. It's not even to be as busy as possible. It is primarily the desire to be creative and a strong will to express themselves that drives them. The basic needs of freedom and self-realization are at the forefront. The other three of the five basic human needs—social belonging, safety and health—are of secondary importance. But they do not disappear and like to make themselves heard in crises. For artists this means a special field of tension, because at first sight seemingly irreconcilable goals are at odds with each other. Now you might say: "So what? I'm all about freedom and self-realization, and that's what I'm aligning myself with." However, that would mean you would be operating past your humanity alongside being an artist. And that will avenge itself sooner or later. The opportunity—both for you as a person and for your to-do list as a performer—is to openly approach this contradiction and take stock: Which of these needs is currently being met or overused in your life, and to what degree? How does this affect your resources and the "question of meaning"? And what new approaches for shaping your life result from this? From my consulting work I know that for everyone working in the creative industry these questions arise in the course of life. The crisis offers you to do it now—even though you might have come to this point later on your own. Every crisis requires us to leave familiar territory. This can have a nice side effect, because newness also activates our reward system. So, by looking at your need for safety, health and social belonging, you can provide both a boost of energy and an update to your answer to the question of meaning. Both will help you tackle the unchanged to-do list for your job with renewed vigor.

The motivational model that is right for you may be different depending on your stage of life and your mood of the day. Self-marketing requires your commitment on many levels—mental, physical, financial, time, analytical, communication, social, creative. It can't hurt to identify and occasionally refresh different pillars for your drive.

After the engine, we now turn to the appropriate habitat for you.

## References

Maslow, Abraham. (1943). *A theory of human motivation.* Psychological Review, 50*(4), 370–396.*

Tarr Krüger, Irmtraud (1993) *Lampenfieber. Ursachen, Wirkung, Therapie.* Stuttgart: Kreuz Verlag.

# Where Is My Habitat?: No More "How Do I Have to Be?"

I assume the purchase or borrowing of this book has been linked to a good resolution for you to take up the subject of self-marketing for the first time or again? Good intentions are for seekers of knowledge and the ambitious. Also a sign of optimism. And idealism. Good resolutions are part of the new year. Likewise to a creative life that is always changing. Whether it's new directions, new developments, new ideas or new challenges, new photos or a new website: Creatives have valuable things to contribute to the topic of good resolutions because they are experts at new beginnings. Ultimately, good intentions are nothing more than newly set goals. Creating new input from yourself during periods of utter helplessness is a remarkable feat. When you fall into the trap of feeling apocalyptic, losing purpose your head will be full of questions like:

- Is it worth it?
- Why didn't that work?
- What am I doing wrong?
- Who should I believe?
- How long can I keep this up?

Impressively reliable, the creative engine starts up again at some point and artists get going again. Driven by a mysterious substance that is peculiar to them and is still too often explained in a clichéd way:

- They just want to be loved.
- They've all got a screw loose.
- Narcissists are always about themselves.

Freely according to the postcard motto "Fall down. Get up. Straighten your crown. Keep going.", creatives get excited again and realize projects that seemingly no one was waiting for. If these products win prizes at some point, they suddenly trigger delight and respect. In my consulting work, I have been able to witness and enjoy this perpetual motion machine time and again. It is all the more regrettable when the questioning and doubting phase reaches an unbearable level. It is of existential importance for artists' souls to feel that they are right. Right for the task, right for the team, right as a human being. In the right place. If they feel wrong, the engine grinds to a halt. Then it says in huge letters on their forehead, "Why can't I be different? I am wrong for my job."

Here is a story about this. I heard a lecture by the doctor and comedian Eckard von Hirschhausen at a congress. The topic of the congress was not creative professions, but the development of potential. He told about how he once looked at a penguin in a Norwegian zoo: "*What a poor sausage! Penguins—too small wings, stocky stature and somehow the creator forgot their knees. Faulty design. Sure.*" He watched the penguin leap into the water, moving agilely, elegantly, and with extraordinary efficiency. "*Penguins are excellent swimmers. They swim 2000 km on the energy from a litre of petrol—that's better than anything humans have ever built.*

*And I thought it was badly constructed!"* Imagine a white circle on a white background and then on a black: how well you fit into your environment, influences to a decisive degree, how competent, how welcome, how right or wrong you feel or are judged by others. Von Hirschhausen says, *"If you were born a penguin, even seven years of psychotherapy won't make you a giraffe. And if you always think 'But I should be like the others', a little consolation: There are already enough others. All that's required of us is to know each other and see if I'm in the right environment for it. And if I'm a penguin and I'm in the desert, it's not my fault if things don't work out."*

> You can recognize the right habitat for you by the fact that problems disappear into thin air.

Singers and musicians can understand this well when they think about the acoustics of a room. If the acoustics inhibit, promote, or color the sound and the propagation of the sound waves in a way that is not conducive to the music, they are powerless. If, on the other hand, they are in the right room, the sounds suddenly unfold into the best possible sound without any effort. Or let's be mundane: every clothing company follows certain standards and fits. Some fit your body better than others. And so, regardless of the outfit, you may present yourself as a "misfit" in one store, but a model in the clothing store next door. What would have happened if there was no store next door? Depending on where you stand, it will significantly affect your self-image.

Leila talks about what it feels like to try to compensate for the lack of fit with a "fake me."

### Leila, 39

*I'm turning forty in a few months, which no one but my family and a few close friends know, because in my resume, like so many others (especially female colleagues), I may not turn forty until I'm fifty. So far, I've always justified it by saying that in this business, you automatically start lying. But it's getting ridiculous, don't you think?*

### Alina Gause

Sometimes I ask clients their age and then explicitly again their true age. Since I am bound by confidentiality, they tell me (probably), but only after some hesitation. The crazy thing is, it starts in the mid-twenties and even the male colleagues are not immune to it. You call it ridiculous, I call it wrong. After all, artistic work is often about truthfulness, and how are you supposed to be authentic if you deny years of your life?

But your question touches on a central aspect that artists in search of work encounter again and again: "How honest can I be? Should I answer the question 'What have you been doing for the last few years?' 'I've been trying to do projects that satisfy me that you've probably never heard of.' 'I'm a single parent. Do you really want to know about my day-to-day life?' 'Little to nothing.' or: 'Murder Mystery Dinner.'?"

Behind this is the recurring question of how far one allows oneself to be defined by business. I have come to the conclusion that in the current job market it is not worth following the so-called laws of business. Who still guarantees you shooting days or a permanent engagement or even an audition or casting because you have dutifully complied with all the requirements? No one. Then why not consistently go your own way? You are at the beginning of the second half of your life. Exactly the right time to set a new course. Why did you go into this profession back then? What plans do you still want to realize? What could still help you grow?

The other day, an actor told me she'd been dreaming of putting together a singing program for years. The main thing stopping her was the worry that people would say about her, "Another actor who thinks she has to sing now, too." That could be arbitrarily replaced with "directing, writing a book, studying, promoting a charitable project,

> teaching." Don't let it stop you: Make sure the next 40 years are filled with life. And stand by it outwardly. I can't imagine it hurting you professionally. On the contrary.
>
> The singer Anastacia became over 10 years older within 1 year. I don't know if that was related to her cancer. I sincerely hope that she was just tired of not being herself.

Whether you allow yourself to be defined by external guidelines or shape the environment to suit your personality has a direct effect on your drive. The more you can act within your ideal habitat, the less friction loss you have to compensate for, and accordingly your power plant is in better shape.

> Fit is the magic word. Invest where you are "more right" than elsewhere.

With the following exercise you will get a first picture of what a living space looks like that concentrates or drains your energies.

> **Exercise Habitat**
> 1. Create two columns on a sheet of paper.
> 2. On the one hand, you collect key points about what motivates you, gives you confidence, promotes you, inspires you, drives you, stimulates you, encourages you, puts you in a positive mood. This means situations, atmospheres, all kinds of sensory impressions, but also people, thoughts and actions. Privately and artistically.
> 3. On the other hand, note influences that inhibit you, discourage you, hinder you, drain your strength, lead you away from yourself.

> 4. Add to the list bit by bit as new aspects occur to you.
> 5. Now comes the hard part: take seriously what you have written down. Increase the influence of what makes your life and actions easier and decrease the destructive influences. Of course, there are external constraints that stand in your way on the way to the ideal living space. However, I know from counseling that there is usually more leeway available in the design of this than you initially assume.

In the introduction to this book, I described the secret of successful self-marketing as being revealed when you are welcome wherever you offer yourself. You could also say: look for the appropriate environment—the place where you automatically feel a bit more "right" than anywhere else. This benefits you for two reasons: first, your counterpart is more likely to also feel that you fit in well there, and so you'll be more likely to find what you're looking for there in terms of career advancement. Secondly, feeling wrong about a place, a task, a role, a social structure invokes another issue that is prevalent and very obstructive for creative personalities when it comes to self-marketing: Shame.

# Shame: No Artistic Flourishing Without Dignity

In my book "Kompass für Künstler" I devote a comparatively short paragraph to the topic of shame. In the meantime, shame, the defense against shame, and the opposite of shame—dignity—are among the central topics for me in my work with creative people, and I therefore address them in more detail in this book. Shame affects whether or not an artist is able to open up to the work, but it is called upon even more strongly when it comes to self-marketing. Two questions are at the heart of this for me:

"Why do creatives so often feel ashamed?"
"Why is this taboo?"

Even before my psychology studies, when I was working exclusively as an artist, these two questions were driving me. However at that time I was so affected by taboo myself that I didn't allow myself the right to feel shame and was only concerned with preventing it. I naturally expected myself, as a professionally trained actor and singer, for example, to overcome my own limitations at the drop of a hat for a role. Or to counter glibly when the ensemble was having a good time at my expense. Or to analyse objectively and soberly when listening to a failed recording. As a psychologist, I then looked into the subject and understood that it is only the other way round that the shoe can fit: Every human being carries shame within him or her. Artists are human beings, but they practise a profession that places great strain on the boundaries of shame. Therefore, they are especially challenged to find a way to deal with it. Not only they themselves, but also all those who guide them in their work. In exploring the sources of shame and the defensive reactions it triggers, I came across a cornucopia of exciting, insightful and useful material for understanding and advising creatives. I am convinced today: If shame and dignity are given sufficient consideration in artistic work contexts, most complications on the way to good results can be sorted out. Therefore, in the following I would like to explore the topic in more depth and give you suggestions on how you can make practical use of it.

Since the American psychologist and researcher Brene Brown became known to a wider audience through her Ted Talk and the translation of her books on vulnerability, people are increasingly concerned with their own shame and vulnerability. Brene Brown (2017) talks about whether someone dares to "step into the arena" or prefers to remain in the protection of invisibility. Artists cannot make this choice because their profession forces them into the arena, so to speak. Yet many manage to retreat, doing damage to themselves and their careers. Sometimes I hear from people seeking advice the phrase, "*I want to come to you because you don't make me feel ashamed.*" By this is meant: for their career choice, for their biography, for their personality, for their plans, ideas, visions and dreams. And that's true. In my rooms, there is no debate about whether it makes sense to be an artist or to want to realize creative ideas. Sometimes that fact alone is enough to break people out of the torpor that shame causes in us and into action. George Bernard Shaw writes, "*We are ashamed of all that is real about us; we are ashamed of ourselves, our relatives, our incomes, our accents, our opinions, our experiences, just as we are ashamed of our naked skin."* (1984). For creatives, this also means:

> Where things get artistically exciting, the greatest shame lurks.

Shame researcher Stephan Marks describes shame as a seismograph that indicates that one of these four basic needs has been violated:

1. Recognition,
2. Protection,
3. Belonging and
4. Integrity.

Marks writes: *"The four themes of shame are like a mobile above a child's cot that every person must rebalance in every situation. Respecting a person's dignity thus means—from the perspective of shame psychology—sparing him or her 'superfluous', avoidable shame: not shaming. It means providing a space in which he or she experiences recognition, protection, belonging, and integrity"*.

> Self-marketing and shame are closely related.

As a particularly creative person, you usually have a vivid connection to your emotional world—and so you are also very conscious of your shame or that of others. Shame interrupts the contact to the environment—and thus behaves contrary to the sense of marketing. When you advertise yourself, for one thing, you have to "out" yourself to the maximum, i.e., leave your protective space to become visible. This potentially puts you at risk of shame. On the other hand, self-marketing primarily means communication, which in turn is not possible at the moment of shame. Here's why: normally, our sympathetic nervous system (the part of the autonomic nervous system responsible for performance) and our parasympathicus (the part of the autonomic nervous system responsible for recovery) alternate in their activity. At the moment of shame, however, they switch to a mode that is actually impossible: they fire simultaneously. As a result, we become incapable of action. We are flooded with shame and can no longer make ourselves understood. Interestingly, the mere observation (within a radius of up to 30 m) of this is enough for us to be ashamed ourselves. So it could be said: shame—like other feelings, by the way—is contagious. You can imagine how this plays out in artistic work contexts when a member of the ensemble, orchestra or team is subjected to (too) harsh criticism, for example, or is shown up with a lewd remark. Also, when you go in front of a jury for an audition, an interview, a competition, a casting or a presentation, it is quite possible that it is not your own shame you feel at all, but that of your counterpart that is transferred to you. When things get really bad, both sides are playing "shame ping-pong." How paradoxical—you have come there to be particularly open and communicative at your best, but find yourself in a state that makes it almost impossible for you to do so. I'll go into more detail below about the defensive reactions that shame can invoke. Take this knowledge with you into your everyday life—related to all three personality parts. I am sure that you will be able to make many interesting observations about this—in yourself and in your fellow human beings.

If you want to market yourself successfully, i.e. authentically, continuously and sustainably, you cannot avoid ensuring a balanced relationship between protection, recognition, belonging and integrity.

> The title of this book is "Presenting without Pandering". The difference between the two terms lies in the degree of dignity.

In your search for the ideal environment, you can assess the degree of fit between your personality, your work environment and the market you want to advertise by asking yourself whether everything you need for dignified self-marketing is offered to you there. Or to use Eckart von Hirschhausen's words again: What does the penguin in you need to avoid feeling like a misfit?

**Recognition**
Recognition, like all words, directly triggers associations in us—both good and bad. In this context, it is not so much the praise character that is meant, but the aspect of being perceived. Being seen and being heard. One could say that it is about the recognition of our existence, which is already shown by the fact that eyes are turned towards us or an ear is lent to us. Sometimes this can be understood literally: one singer told of how, during an audition, she stood on stage, the pianist began to play and she began to sing. Meanwhile, in the auditorium, the director, musical director, artistic director, and others present sat noisily opening packages of cookies, talking, laughing, and eating. Recognition can only exist when you are visible and your presence is even noticed. Recognition is therefore directly related to protection.

For example, ask yourself:

- Are you being listened to?
- Do they remember what you said?
- Do they turn their eyes to you?
- Are you getting feedback that relates to you?
- Are changes perceived in you?
- Do they know your name?
- Do they address special circumstances (that you may not be a native speaker, are currently going through a divorce, have children, or are afraid of heights?).
- What makes you personally feel appreciated or when do you feel disregarded?

**Protection**

Creativity is promoted where there is a protective space. Gerald Hüther, one of the leading scientists on the topics of learning and creativity, writes: "*Wherever there is an attempt to exploit existing resources to the utmost, where fear is stoked, pressure is exerted, precise regulations and controls are imposed, where thinking along is not valued and responsibility is not transferred, the creative potential of employees is not only overlooked. It is suppressed*" (2020).

So your personal creativity is not just something to wait for like a muse, but it is variously enabled or inhibited by different environments. A climate where mistakes are forbidden stifles creativity. Much like in a therapeutic setting the real issues are only addressed when there is trust and confidentiality, artists open up best where they can rely on those around them. Since they are professionals, they also open up where there is no protection, but with a great deal of additional energy, which is not without consequences in the long run.

## Shame: No Artistic Flourishing Without Dignity

Protection can be provided from the outside but also from the inside. Protection from the outside is given when your physical and psychological boundaries are respected. You yourself can provide protection from within by, for example, ensuring that you are well prepared, taking moral reinforcement with you depending on the situation and knowing, respecting and defending your personal boundaries yourself. Marketing yourself means venturing out of the protective shadow into the light. To avoid being surprised and hindered by feelings of shame there, it is advantageous to equip yourself well for this.

We are still in the first part and are dedicated to the optimal basic attitude to promote yourself. This includes that your shame-mobile is well balanced.

For example, ask yourself:

- Does your work environment ensure that you can prepare if this is not possible in your genre at home?
- In your opinion, is the work performance expected of you appropriate and feasible?
- Do you get adequate breaks?
- Do you have a consensus amongst colleagues about what constitutes a boundary violation?
- Is it more common within your work for individuals to be shown up in an unpleasant way?
- Is there a feedback culture that suits you?
- Are there points of contact in the event of a legal or other violation?
- Do you sense an effort to create good conditions for creative work?
- What gives you a personal sense of protection or boundary violation?

## Belonging

The group provides protection and orientation, and that strengthens us. Be it the family, the clique, the neighborhood, the regional origin—we like to know where and to whom we belong. Man, the herd animal. That's why it's sometimes not at all easy for artists when they have to separate from environments that have offered a clear sense of belonging. Ensembles, casts, collectives can become second families or replace them altogether. If the engagement was temporary and ends, surprisingly strong feelings of loss and separation can arise. When the need to belong is particularly strained, artistically suboptimal environments sometimes seem more attractive than they actually are. In the case of long-term contracts, this can mean shying away from change. This does not mean a case of weighing different needs well and finding the best possible compromise, such as "It's more important to me to build a family, so I'm happy to stay where I am, even though I would prefer greater challenges in purely artistic terms." Sometimes, out of the need to belong, bad career decisions are made. After all, following one's ideals always carries the risk of loneliness (in addition to insecurity). For example, saying no when doors open that don't suit you artistically. Or to say yes when it comes to daring to make a career leap. In both cases, integrity is required (which I will discuss below) and the need to belong must take a back seat. In order to be independent of this when it comes to important decisions, one can find other ways to gain belonging.

I remember, for example, a performer who went into her first engagements after graduation and was herself overwhelmed by how homesick she was. She was distraught, knowing that extended absences from home and frequent travel would be unavoidable for her professional life. She loved her job, but the homesickness was so strong that she was about to give it up. We discussed ways she could assure herself of belonging in other ways. She noted what strengthened her sense of belonging and took the list seriously: from then on, she spoke in her native dialect outside of work hours and arranged fixed phone times with her closest friends. She had "care packages" sent to her from home and talked more about where she came from and what she missed there (she hadn't allowed herself to do that before). This improved her contact—and thus her sense of belonging—with the rest of the ensemble, and her quality of life increased. At the same time, she took her love of home as an opportunity to do more canvassing in her place of residence so that she could work there more often.

For example, ask yourself:

- Are there common values?
- Do you share the same sense of humor?
- Are birthdays or other holidays significant to everyone?
- Do you shy away from contact outside of work?
- Or, conversely, do you feel they shy away from contacting you?
- Would you say things are generally fair where you are?
- What gives you personally a sense of belonging or exclusion?
- When, where, with whom, what makes you feel at home?

**Integrity**
It would be easy to identify the appropriate habitat for oneself if it were solely about belonging and the aspect of integrity did not exist. But just as protection and recognition are interrelated, integrity and belonging are interdependent. The more one professes to belong to a grouping, the less one may be able to follow one's own personal convictions and inclinations. The pressure not to violate one's own

values can lead to disengagement from a group or to exclusion. This is a familiar tension for artists: how much can I tolerate that is not in line with my values until I drop out of a production? There is no point in self-marketing that contradicts one's own values.

Ask yourself:

- Do you feel like you have to deny yourself in your work?
- Does it often happen that you keep silent in order not to offend?
- Do you notice too often for your taste that your opinion is not asked for?
- Do you feel you have to conform on key issues in order not to be excluded?
- When do you personally feel that you can act in accordance with your most important beliefs or that your values are being violated?

I would like to remind you once again why these topics are essential for your self-marketing: Dealing with your own feelings of shame will determine whether your plan to venture out and offer yourself is promising or doomed to failure. The—as Stephan Marks calls it—"shame mobile" of belonging, recognition, protection and integrity needs to be well balanced in order to get into the right starting position for your self-marketing. Shame triggers shame defense reactions. And these defensive reactions sabotage you in your quest to promote yourself. Feeling shame is so uncomfortable that your inner self won't care if you've read the right books and planned everything well, not even if your professional livelihood depends on it: At the first sign of shame, your "reptilian brain" takes over and you run away, hide, or rebel.

Shame defense reactions can be summarized into three groups:

1. **Hide**
   Including for example, emotional numbness, bunking off, but also hiding behind masks—mimicing or through exaggerated make-up.
2. **Attack**
   This can show itself in the shaming and contempt of others, in cynicism, shamelessness, negativism, arrogance, all forms of aggression, envy or defiance.
3. **Escape**
   In fantasies of grandeur, idealization, perfectionism, silliness, addiction, or puzzlement. Or simply literal escape, that is, leaving the shameful situation.

One of the reasons why it is so important that you find or design the right living space for you is that it offers you the best possible circumstances to reduce feelings of shame, and therefore defensive reactions, to a minimum. Find out what that means for you personally. What makes you feel ashamed? Go on a research trip and analyze what triggers it. Was it unavoidable in the specific situation or was your shame unnecessarily provoked? Did you already bring some of it from home? Also take a look around: you will surely recognize when your colleagues feel ashamed and activate defensive reactions. Perhaps you are sitting together in the waiting room of a casting, audition, competition, interview or presentation and a fellow competitor is constantly engaging them in conversation to create a sense of belonging? Or a competitor conveys quite clearly in her arrogant expression that, from her perspective, you are worlds apart?

Julian, who wrote to me, is a good example of how treacherous it can be when the four aspects of the mobile have fallen short. He is looking for belonging, for his own values, and for recognition. As a result, he is often confronted with shame and shame defense in the form of envy, for which he then feels additional shame—a painful cycle.

### Julian, 32

*I'm afraid I have to make a terrible statement about myself: I am consumed by envy. And I suffer from it. It gets to the point where I blush when I'm standing with several colleagues and someone else is being praised. Not to mention when I hear that someone has found a good agency or been cast on a great project. I don't watch awards ceremonies anymore because I'm in a bad mood for days afterwards. I think it's a pathetic attitude myself and I want to change it. But how?*

### Alina Gause

In addition to the unpleasant feeling of envy, you also have a good dose of self-accusation—which no one can bear for long. If we understand envy as a variable process that has its source somewhere, then rises, develops into resentment, and finally leads to a desire to actively harm others, you personally are not even halfway down the potentially possible path. This is as far as you are likely to go on this path—and this is the good news. You seem to be protected from this by a natural defensive attitude: you understand that envy harms you first and foremost, and so you want to detach yourself from it. How it would sound if you gave it free rein? *"Maybe it's just not your thing, the part." "I know someone who did the format, he can't get a leg up now." "I think what XY said about you the other day was impossible." "All the good ones are fleeing your agency." "You didn't hear it from me, but I think he has a drinking problem."* So go ahead and give yourself a quick pat on the back for not being able to reconcile this behavior with your self-image. But now to the source of your envy. Envy arises where an important inner pot is (too) empty. So your envy keeps pointing out that you are missing something. What we humans envy others for varies from era to era. If in the past it was the abundance of children and then material goods—today it is

> more likely to be a fulfilled, social life. Or another good, which envy researcher Rolf Haubl considers to be a particularly coveted good of our time: Orientation, or a fixed order in life. This is something that the acting profession tends not to offer. The few orientation variables we have are, for example: Agencies, contracts or prizes. So I'm not surprised that it's those very things you mention. To reduce your feelings of envy to a tolerable level, you could try to fill the "orientation pot" on your own. To do this, try to determine at what point you are particularly disoriented: In the direction of your career? In the assessment of your abilities or your effect on others? In your role as a marketer? In your general life goals? A little bit of everything? Ask yourself, ask friends, relatives and, if necessary, professionals who can offer guidance in the areas where you need it. This will reveal how you can regain more order and thus stability and ultimately a more stable sense of self. Fill your self-esteem pot with knowledge about yourself, your goals and your means. With initiative and conviction. You will see that the fuller your pot is, the easier it will be for you to be generous. It's a feeling you're sure to like. And should you ever envy someone fiercely again, remember Wilhelm Busch—"*Envy is the sincerest form of recognition*"—and indulge your competitor.

Jonas goes on to describe very vividly how shame is triggered by the withdrawal of belonging. What is fatal about this is the self-affirming cycle that it triggers.

### Jonas, 33

*I'm shooting for a series right now and within a few days I've become the idiot of the team. I know this from other productions: there was always someone who was too stupid, too slow, too stiff or too untalented. Now it's supposed to be me? All I can say is: that's me. I can't remember my lines, always getting in someone's way, always making mistakes. And then the vicious cycle begins: I feel ashamed, get even less on the line, feel even more ashamed, and so on. I want to get out of it—how do I do that?*

### Alina Gause

Shame is a widespread and far too little appreciated phenomenon among creative personalities. It is regrettable that so little work is done with this feeling, as it can explain many blockades and conflicts in artistic teams. Apparently, performers are not granted the right to be ashamed. Artists, especially performers—so it is thought—must be brazen, willing and happy to show off at any time. In fact they are ordinary people who, like everyone else, feel ashamed when they are deprived of any of these four elements: Recognition, protection, belonging or integrity. Are you the "jerk of the team?" Then you have been stripped of belonging to the group. The others have thus reassured themselves of their own belonging a little more. You're going to embarrass yourself with every new mistake? Then you lack protection. If you had been granted a sense of belonging or protection at the moment of a mistake, you would not have fallen into the vicious circle. If we are ashamed, we inevitably become losers. Let me explain why: at the moment of shame, our autonomic system collapses because both sympathetic and parasympathetic systems are firing. Normally, they alternate—the former takes care of our performance, the latter takes care of the recovery phases. And now neither of them knows what is needed. The result: we become incapacitated. We are flooded with shame and can no longer make ourselves understood. You just noticed that: the inability to act manifests itself in further embarrassment and the vicious circle is perfect. What you can do now is: first of all, accept that shame—similar to stage fright—cannot or should not be abolished, but that it is a matter of keeping it at a bearable level. To do that, make sure the four elements above are present in good balance. Feeling defenseless? Provide yourself with protection—before, after and on the set, for example, by being calm, focused and encouraged by well-meaning people. This will reduce the margin for error. Belonging and recognition are harder to obtain on your own in this case, but will follow. On a side note, you mentioned that you know other "chosen idiots" from previous productions? Now you'll understand that just like the king, "the idiot" doesn't play itself, but needs the group to do so. Maybe keep that in mind the next time you're about to breathe a sigh of relief because you're on "the safe side."

We differ in our levels of offendibility. How quickly shame is triggered in us depends on how often we have experienced that our boundaries or values have been violated, that we have been disregarded or rejected. If our measure is basically already full, even weak stimuli ("I think the longer hair looked better on you.") can trigger an overflow of shame. In this case, it takes more intense processing of these experiences to expose ourselves to the cold waters of business. The bad news is: in order to venture out into the marketplace and offer, a certain amount of shame is unavoidable. It's similar to stage fright, which is just as much not to be abolished as it is to be adjusted to the right temperature. There is also good news: dealing with this topic will advance you privately, artistically and also in marketing matters.

## References

Brown, Brene (2017). *Verletzlichkeit macht stark*. München: Wilhelm Goldmann Verlag.

Hüther, Gerald (2020). https://kulturwandel.org/inspiration/interviews-und-texte/wie-gehirngerechte-fuhrungfunktioniert/ Stand 18.4.2020.

Shaw, George Bernard (1984). Mensch und Übermensch.

# Overcoming the "Ouch Complex": Feeling Good Is a Must

In order to find the right habitat for oneself, one must first be able to claim that something can be pleasant and easy. That enduring pain and overcoming particularly difficult obstacles are not necessary prerequisites for legitimizing oneself as an artist.

> Creatives often find it surprisingly difficult to invest their energy not where rejection lurks, but where already open doors can be opened even wider.

Not caring for fans, but having to refute the harshest criticism. Not to care for waterways as a penguin, but to travel the desert. Perhaps you know this? I paraphrase this attitude common among many creatives with the term "Ouch Complex" = "Only when it hurts, when it's hard, can it be right. No pain no gain." This is harmful nonsense. Coming face to face with yourself and your own limitations hurts enough. Instead, artists need a comfortable and dignified field to unfold around them, where they can follow their own convictions and free themselves bit by bit. Then they will be at their best.

### Philipp, 30

*The other day it happened that I was working with a new acting coach. I felt comfortable throughout, never felt like I was being pushed back to my limits. It was all straightforward and smooth. The problem only arose afterwards when I became skeptical: Was her positive feedback honest or nicely colored? Was she challenging me enough? Did she make it too easy for herself and me? I'm considering going back to a coach next time who will challenge me more critically. Does that make sense?*

### Alina Gause

It's not uncommon for me to see creatives seeking appreciation where it's difficult rather than where it succeeds without much friction. I call this the "Ouch Complex"—"only when it hurts is it good". Many artists can't believe that what is most interesting and artistically productive about them is themselves. That which "just comes out" of them. Instead, they want to accomplish something, work hard, then a harvest seems appropriately earned. So, many direct their interest to where there is resistance to overcome: particularly merciless critics, the family member who least believes in success, tasks that are outside their comfort zone. Fans are welcome, but appear as dubious recognition and are not taken seriously. It is a paradox that weakens them: on the one hand, the belief that "those who are really good will be found and courted" or those who have to look for support (from agencies, audiences, financiers, press ...) are exposed as talentless. On the other hand, "This support came too smoothly, it can't be worth anything. I have to convince those who don't want me." In this way, there is too little courting of those willing to support, and helpful offers are allowed to pass by. To prevent this from happening, enthusiasm, time and effort should be recognized and valued as the ultimate cachet in career guides and mentors, and these relationships should be cherished. Sometimes an eye, an ear or a window of time opens for just a moment. It is important to recognize this moment through the confusion of half-hearted, dishonest, hasty, superficial or even destructive signals. Take a look around: maybe the young up-and-coming agent who's been chasing you for a while is the more interesting address than the established agency that hasn't responded to you in months? Maybe the 12 fans who are sometimes the only audience at one of your shows right now aren't taste-struck losers, but the start of something? Maybe the grandma who's currently funding your workshop in LA isn't to be pitied, but ends up being the one you mention in your acceptance speech? And don't worry: it won't prevent challenges—they're included in your career choice either way. It just saves you the detour of explaining yourself and convincing others that you're worth investing in. You leave the side building sites and deal directly with the most difficult critic you can't get rid of anyway: yourself.

### Theo, 28

*Actually, I shouldn't complain because as an actor I can make a living from my shooting days. Nevertheless, I am dissatisfied because I know that there is much more to me than what I show at auditions. In workshops and trainings I always hear that I am blocked and that I can't reach my full potential. I'm tired of being underestimated and overlooked because of it. How do I move forward?*

### Alina Gause

You address an aspect that is one of the most common reasons creatives contact me. Artists tend to doubt themselves when they see unsatisfactory results. They are often supported in this by their professional environment: there is quickly talk of blockages, a lack of willingness to devote oneself, being "stuck in one's head" or uptight. This is also the reason why they are willing to invest a lot in order to eliminate these supposed incompetencies. In doing so, however, creatives sometimes set in motion a counterproductive cycle: they seek out offers to get better. These, in turn, build on wanting to effect positive change, which requires that something be identified as suboptimal beforehand. In the best case, a satisfactory development is achieved. However,

> it is also possible that a problem is dealt with that is not a problem at all—at least not an urgent one. The people concerned, however, now plunge into the next measure, etc., in the certainty that they are getting closer to the core of their deficiency. In this way they weaken their most important and at the same time most fragile resource: their self-confidence. A client once aptly said to me: "*How good do I actually still have to become?*"
>
> In my experience, it is predominantly hurdles other than the mastery of new techniques that artists have to overcome in order to be able to call on their full potential, of which I would like to mention only the most important: stage fright, being underchallenged, artistic differences and an uneasy working atmosphere. Nick Nolte once said, when asked what advice he would give to the young generation of actors, "*Don't squat around in acting classes, not as patient extras, but act, in what medium doesn't matter at all ... You die umpteen times before you step on stage. But then you celebrate resurrection ... It's a wonderful art form, this circling around the core of a play, this rotating around a role that you work on day and night. Sometimes I wake up at night and think: Oh, that was fantastic! That's exactly how I'm going to do it! And the next day I try it—and I usually flunk it. Where else in life am I allowed to do that?*" (SZ from March 22, 2012).
>
> With this in mind, find tasks that you take so seriously that you want to burn for them, surround yourself with people who motivate you to perform at your best, and set your stage fright to the right temperature. Then chances are very good that you won't be overlooked.

Possibly you had the thought while reading: "The right habitat—if it were so easy! I'd jump right in, but they won't let me!". Yes, they will let you. But for that to happen, you have to be recognizable—you have to match in style, orientation, attitude, commitment, and competencies what they are looking for where you would like to be a member. If you stand outside the heavy metal club dressed in a Bavarian dirndl, it's possible you'll be denied affiliation. It won't do for you to say you just quickly grabbed what was hanging in the closet—the studded pants were just at the cleaners and the black eyeliner pencil just happened to run out, too. I'm aware of how hard access points are to achieve in the artistic firmament. They are guarded by gatekeepers who pride themselves on debunking any disguise and want to keep their club exclusive. That's only unfair if it's based on incompetence, a blind claim to truth, or a lust for power. In many cases, however, it stems from a genuine love of one's profession. Anyone who has invested many years of blood, sweat and tears in their art thoroughly checks whether someone seeking access is at the right operating temperature for it. When casting directors, gallery owners, directors, musical directors or agencies sift through hundreds of application materials, they develop a good eye for who writes a mass email, considers photos with an out-of-date hair length or unglued sheet music sufficient and who does not. Artists often feel like perpetual supplicants and want to avoid giving a begging impression at all costs. In doing so, they overlook the fact that with every note they practice, every journey they take, every investment in an outstanding result, they also earn a right of belonging.

> Show your club that you belong.

Show that you can be relied upon, that you can be trusted with a role, a part, an exhibition, a presentation, a production. Show what commitment you have made up to this point and what you are still prepared to do in the future. Take yourself seriously in your request and you will be taken seriously. As an artist, you have probably already succeeded in this. Only in self-marketing perhaps not yet with the same conviction? This is not a task you should ask your creative self to do. Your *Third Person* will take over from now on.

# Help Is at Hand: Discover Your *Third Person*

I first wrote about my concept of "The Three Personality Parts of Creative People" in my book "Kompass für Künstler". I see in it a meaningful thought model for creatives to use their different personality parts more efficiently and sustainably for a satisfying life design. I wasn't surprised that it generated the most interest of all the concepts I described. I interpreted this as a sign of how much the topic of self-marketing weighs on creative personalities and, moreover, how gratefully they take up approaches that depict them as total personalities and in which the artistic aspect is not overlooked.

> The first, the second and the *Third Person*—not a multiple personality disorder, but the dream team of creative personalities.

The artistic profession differs from most other professions in the intersection of personal and professional space: where does leisure end and work begin? Is it possible not to take rejection personally when only one's own person is being evaluated? Artistic ensembles are often perceived as family; content of work must be personally meaningful. Not singing, playing, drawing, designing, painting, creating, writing, expressing oneself means for many artists not feeling alive. There are many advantages to densely combining one's person with one's professional activity: the work is fun, you can't get enough of it, it lasts a lifetime, and much more. However, if there is a problem or if you want to change or improve something, the reverse is also true: it triggers a conflagration. All strengths and weaknesses, difficulties and successes are in one pot. This makes it confusing and leads to the fact that in case of dissatisfaction you cannot determine exactly what is causing it. In order to create a better overview here, to formulate more targeted approaches to solutions and not to overlook anything, I have created the framework of the three personality parts, which need to be provided with regard to their different needs, but also with specific attitudes and tasks.

**The First Person**
It combines all personality traits, needs, life circumstances, preferences, interests, skills, sore points and experiences that concern your private person. Your marital status, your origin, your current life reality, but also your food and holiday preferences, whether you like animals, like to collect stamps or knit scarves.

The first person gets along. Even when she is not coping, it is as a living consequence of a situation, a phase or an event. She is not well when she is burdened, she is annoyed when she does not succeed at something, she may also be overtired, beside herself or at a loss as to how to classify something. However all that is a part of her and therefore authentic. Her behaviour is a mirror of her personality—this may not always be pleasant for her and those around her, but the private person is made up of an infinite number of shades and with each additional year of life experience she gets to know these facets better. By the time she enters vocational training or professional life, she has been on the road with herself for many years. The experiential knowledge that has arisen in the process is available to her.

**The Second Person**
It is activated the moment you practice your art. It is not crucial where this is the case—whether in the workshop, in the living room, on stage, in the studio or in nature. But it does matter that it only affects the moments when you are immersed in artistic activity. This is significant in that the second person is in an extraordinary state of consciousness during that time. There's even a legal component to this—it's possible for an artist to be granted just before or just after a performance that they cannot be held fully responsible for their actions. Immersed in the activity, you lose your sense of time, no hunger, thirst or pain arise. You are concentrated, tense and relaxed at the same time (in my book "Warum Künstler die glücklicheren Menschen sein könnten" I go into detail about this "flow" described by Mihaly Csikszentmihalyi). Another feature of this creative state is its nurturing aspect. The second person is able to add energy to the overall trio of first, second and *Third Person*.

The second person—your creative self—also gets along. She draws, sings, plays, invents, photographs, learns texts, rehearses, designs, creates, presents. This can also be done better or worse, but she works purposefully based on existing skills. If mistakes happen or her work is not appreciated, the despair is great, but a natural consequence indicating a rich life. She is also congruent with the situation. She is intensely concerned with being able to assess and meet requirements and continues to expand her knowledge pool through each experience. Therefore, she is happy about every test. The second person is usually the one who likes to live the most.

## The *Third Person*

The *Third Person* now appears in situations that can neither be assigned to your private person nor to you at the moment of performing a creative activity. Typical examples are the agency's brunch, the anteroom of a casting or audition, premiere parties, private parties with professionally interesting people, the brief conversation with the director who asks to get to know you before shooting begins, trade fairs, alumni meetings or chance encounters with potential employers.

As a rule, the *Third Person* is the runt of the litter. Schematically put on and not very socially competent. She feels like she is walking on eggs or thin ice. She has little self-reflection and is usually one-sided in her negative evaluations. She prefers to sit at home where she doesn't have to face anyone or do anything. This wouldn't be a problem if the *Third Person* wasn't your only communicator in business.

> Employers talk exclusively to your *Third Person*.

The private person exists only in private contexts and the stage person cannot speak at all (as, for example, in the visual arts or in the field of words and graphics) or only professionally (as, for example, in the field of acting or presenting). The *Third Person* is the contact person. Related to the topic of this book, you could also say: your *Third Person* is the one who is responsible for your self-marketing.

The concept of the three personality parts arose from an observation for which I was looking for a name. Creative people usually have a rich inner life full of feelings, convictions, visions, ideas and plans. This makes them exciting conversation partners who can win others over with their charisma, passion, temperament, enthusiasm and unconventional thinking. It is all the more amazing to see them undergo a metamorphosis in a matter of seconds when they are asked to promote themselves. All of a sudden, it seems as if they have trouble giving their arms a suitable task, formulating coherent sentences without "somehow" or just being friendly. You'd think they barely know their stuff and their memory leaves something to be desired. Some *Third Person* leaves the impression that the last thing they would care about is working in their profession. Now it's one thing to fail at the job of being an advertiser. It is another, however, if the *Third Person* shows herself from a side that is particularly bad in terms of character. For example, if she talks down to the second person (the artist ego):

> "Look at her! She obviously belongs here while you are just an embarrassment!"
> "Everything he touches turns to gold. Can't exactly say the same for you…"
> "Long time no hear from you … Are you actually still around or can I retire?"
> "You're not serious about me offering this stuff, are you? I'm not going to make a fool of myself because of you. Produce something decent before you send me out there."
> "Unimaginative, incoherent drivel."
> "How about medical school?"
> "Your parents were right."
> "You're so ordinary."
> "You seriously want to compete with the others in the market?"

In this worst case, the *Third Person* sabotages the whole trio. In the best case—and this is what we are aiming for—the *Third Person* manages your three personality parts as one would wish: she takes care of the three "little horses" as best as she can in order to be able to motivate them to peak performance at the right moment. She makes sure that there are realistic and productive work and recovery sessions for each personality part. This requires to-do lists and not-to-do lists, goals, training and lots of encouragement. If she does her job really well, the *Third Person* keeps the long view and pursues a sustainable career. That's why she makes sure that none of the three areas is neglected for too long: neither private life, nor art, nor marketing.

Dennis' life situation illustrates the importance of first, second and *Third Person* not working against each other but pulling together.

---

**Dennis, 26**

*I'm gay. Only my two closest friends know that, though. If I'm asked directly, I lie, because I'm convinced it will hurt me as an actor—but will it? Not showing it is a high price to pay because it never really makes me feel alive. Do you know others who feel the same way? What would you do if you were me?*

**Alina Gause**

Yes, unfortunately I know others who feel the same way. Many think that the artistic profession is a place where no one has to worry about being open about their sexual orientation. It isn't. Performers have to be careful with personal information (age, medical conditions, marital status) because they know they will also be booked as a projection screen and personal information will trigger associations. So you ask yourself: do they still trust me to be the heterosexual lover then? Does this narrow my role profile to the point that there are no offers for me in the already tight job market? I won't be able to give you a clear answer to that—more of a decision-making guide.

I see a three-way split with creatives: there's you as a private person, then there's you as a stage person, and finally there's a *Third Person* who shows up when a situation isn't clearly professional or private (like in the front office of an audition or at the agency brunch). Each of these three personality parts has a different opinion about your question. The stage person has no interest in coming out, she plays the roles she is given and wants to be as unrestricted as possible. What about the private person? She wants to live openly gay and finds the "price too high". The *Third Person* wrote to me. She is the one who mediates between the other two and represents you to the outside world. She has to decide and since the *Third Person* is usually the most insecure in that trio, we need to empower her for that decision. A casting director saying I once heard—"The moment you leave the apartment, you are no longer private."—is understandable, and yet, if you think it through, it's unhealthy. It constricts them too much in an area that is the source of their artistic creation and turns them into puppets of the business.

It is similar with your question: where will it ultimately lead if you deny yourself? Your private person is the one who falls in love, is sometimes ill, likes licorice or not, collects experiences and develops convictions. That's what makes them up and from that they feed your stage persona. Your *Third Person* has to decide by process of elimination: 'I don't know what the consequences will be if I come out. But I know what there will be if I don't. Can I live with that?' Perhaps coming out will not only block paths for you (if at all), but open up new ones? The stage person, the private person and the *Third Person* are all very powerful together. Creatives had better tap into that source—in your case, for a clear stance, "I'm an actor—and that's fine."

So everything you've read so far has ultimately been directed at your *Third Person*.

The *Third Person* is the one we want to discover with this book, to whom we want to give the back and the responsible task of your self-marketing to spare your artist self with it. It is completely irrelevant whether your *Third Person* is talented or pre-trained for this. She is part of the family and therefore we assume that she wants your best and is willing to learn and do whatever is necessary to achieve it.

As I have already explained, the first and the second person are usually several steps ahead of the third. They are familiar with their area and each other. They know their strengths and weaknesses quite well and take turns without much friction. They know ways and means to accomplish their respective tasks or are working on them. The *Third Person*, on the other hand, is more often than not the one who lacks attitude, specific tasks, and work ethic because they receives less attention. This omission manifests itself in insecurity and awkwardness, because even if little attention is paid to her, she still has to constantly prove herself on the floor of self-marketing. If she is not adequately prepared for this, it increases the likelihood of feelings of shame, and this in turn results in the defensive reactions already mentioned.

In the following chapter I go into more detail about this "Vicious Circle of Self-Marketing" and present you with the "Angelic Ladder of Self-Marketing". We take care to provide your *Third Person* with concrete tasks and to let her gain self-confidence about them. For this you only have to do one thing: get into action.

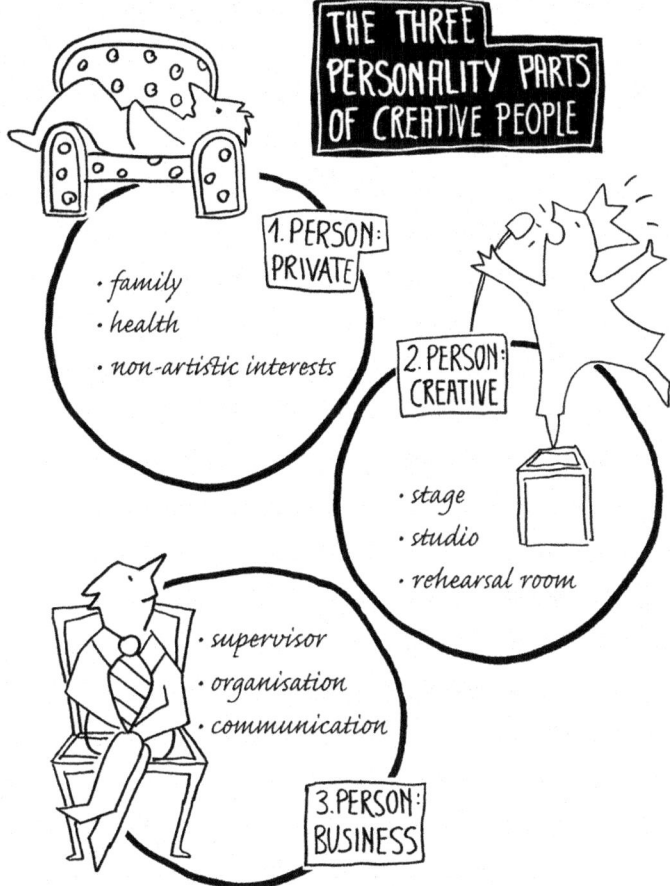

The Three Personality Parts of Creative People

# Part II

## Get into Action

Concrete action strengthens what is described in psychology with the word "self-efficacy": the conviction that we can achieve something through our own efforts. To put it another way: whether we trust ourselves to successfully bring our plans to the finish line. It is obvious that someone who thinks he or she has little chance of achieving something on his or her own initiative will also invest little—in terms of time, vision, money and energy. On the other hand, those who have had the experience that their actions also lead to something will be able to persevere even when there are setbacks.

> Self-efficacy can be learned or strengthened.

There is a very simple recipe for this: doing. Words can motivate you, but lasting conviction is more likely to come from the results of your own actions. They are stored like a multi-dimensional image in your body, mind and soul as a convincing experience. Then one day when you set out on your next hero's journey, the confidence in your undertakings is already a layer thicker and it is a bit easier for you to take each new step. Therefore we want you to get into action and thus strengthen your self-efficacy. So that you do not shy away from difficult hurdles.

**Get into Action**

Take the film market, for example: the casting process in Germany is more inaccessible and intransparent than in almost any other country. The market is overcrowded—access is very selective and often procured through relationships. The effect is that we tend to see the same faces and may wonder whether this is due to the unique quality of all of them. So we're dealing with a market where it's easy to doubt that initiative and activity can make any difference at all—but it does. Only with appropriate input, though, in a particularly inaccessible market. The harder it gets the harder you try. Performers who have been able to establish themselves in the film and television market without family contacts or a film vita built up since childhood and adolescence tell me that they work full-time. However, they are not talking about acting, but about their *Third Person*. This is because they rarely shoot more than 30 days a year out of their total working hours (soap operas excepted). What a ratio between acting and marketing! You can't blame anyone for refusing to put in the effort. Again, everyone knows what to do or where to get the necessary information, but very few *do* it. Those that do, get where they want to go. At the beginning of my consulting work I would have been more cautious with this statement, but for over 10 years I have been asking all the artists I work with what they have invested and harvested. This means not only financial aspects, but also temporal, emotional, visionary, artistic or personal. I also ask what outcomes are due to the engagement of others—for example, the agency. There is a clear correlation between the amount of input and the output. Therefore, the goal of this book is for you to increase your input, but also that you use your resources as efficiently as possible in the process.

Every now and then I look into a young face and hear myself say, "*You should assume that no one who meets you in this profession is seriously interested in you.*" I'm not saying this out of bitterness or hopelessness, but because I know that those who are most likely to have a self-determined, existentially secure and artistically fulfilled life are those who take responsibility for it themselves. We live (especially in Germany) in a society where culture per se is not given legitimacy. As I noted at the outset, it is treated as a luxury, carried out by people for fun or self-fulfillment, and therefore does not necessarily have to be paid for. This social devaluation does not make artistic professions less attractive, but it does make it more difficult to secure one's livelihood. This in turn increases the need for self-marketing. Creatives should be aware that their decision to follow this career path is an individual one, the consequences of which—both pleasant and unpleasant—they alone will bear, and that they must rely first and foremost on themselves to achieve their goals. The fact that no one is really interested in them is in this respect only meant to express pointedly how important it is to develop a keen eye and a special appreciation for the exceptions to this rule from the very beginning and to take care responsibly of the part that is in one's own hands.

We know from educational psychology that learning is particularly successful when it takes place on different sensory levels. That is, when a child speaks the alphabet, sees it written and then follows it as a map on the floor. Likewise, it is helpful when what is learned is translated into one's own vocabulary and one's own world of thoughts and feelings and is connected to one's personal store of memories. Applied to the topic of this book, this means that after we have been on the way rather intellectually in the first chapter, it is now a matter of connecting the attitude that has arisen with practical, sensual experiences that are personally relevant to you. For this reason, here comes a first concrete task that literally gives you something to do:

> **The book to the book** Please get a pad or a notebook reserved for notes around your self-marketing.

The majority of the artists I know love paper. Of course they use computers with all their technical refinements, and yet they also like to doodle, note, sketch or glue. It's as if these real-life, quasi-creative acts can help the flow of ideas. For many, the term "creative chaos" is an apt description of how perfectly tidy, orderly worlds don't mesh as well with creative flow as doodling and different textures to touch or look at. I'm thinking, for example, of a writer who could be most reliably creative on the commuter train, writing in little notebooks. When she couldn't take her sick dog on public transport for a while and so mainly drove, that significantly affected her writing. Many creatives also love the stories they associate with objects. So notebooks can encourage invention via this emotional patina. Though you might be one of those people who exclusively store words and music digitally and have a spotless apartment where you can eat your dinner off the floor. No matter—please jot down, bullet-point or sprawling (whatever floats your boat) what has, or will, come to mind in your reading. Make notes about it that you will still understand 5 years from now. Ultimately, it is the combination of this book and your personal notes that will produce the most useful guidebook for you—because you are the expert for yourself.

**My first, second and Third Person** Take a moment, pick up your notebook, and write down for
- The first person—your private person,
- The second person—your creative self and
- The *Third Person*—the management of the trio,

what characterizes you in each case and where you currently see a need for action.

For each of the three personality parts within you, ask yourself:
1. What makes you stand out in it? What is typical for you? What would others say about you?
2. What are your strengths and your weaknesses?
3. Which of the weaknesses do you have to accept, which ones would you like to face?
4. What do the different parts of you need in order to feel good, in order to be motivated? When are you at your best?
5. What are you currently missing and why?
6. How could you change that?
7. What can you manage on your own, where do you need support?

There are great individual differences between creatives in the intersections of the three personality parts. In group workshops I sometimes ask participants to visualize the intersections by three circles. Some feel there is little difference between the first, second and *Third Person* states—the circles are almost congruent. Others feel as if they are actually living three different realities of life, the circles just barely touching. Either way, the three personality parts are closely interconnected, build on each other, depend on each other. That is, anything you invest in one part will affect the other parts. The same is true if you neglect aspects.

# The Vicious Circle of Self-Marketing: Why Too Much Market Blocks Creativity

I developed the "Vicious Circle of Self-Marketing" to describe what often lies behind when self-promotion drains and depresses creatives. It starts with the …

**Desire for Success**
Artists want to be seen and heard. They want to establish a connection between their inner world and the outside world through the artistic expression of thoughts and feelings. They usually do this already in their imagination during the creative process. In doing so, they anticipate in their imagination the reaction of their readers and listeners, the spectators. As if they were in love and inwardly anticipating the presence of the beloved, they build hopes and expectations. Many talk about it—coyly or self-deprecatingly—as they sometimes formulate acceptance speeches for awards they are very unlikely to ever receive (and can be bizarrely completely unprepared when it does happen).

Every artist understands success in a different way, but they all share the longing to be recognized in their entire personality, with all their skills and all their content. What this expresses itself in—in the degree of fame, in money, prizes, in the recognition of personally significant people or simply in a good feeling about oneself—can be very different. However, it rarely corresponds to what people who do not pursue an artistic profession understand by it. I never tire of repeating the story of two brothers: Both danced in companies that brought tears of happiness to dancers' eyes. Throughout their professional lives, they were seen on the biggest stages all over the world. They originally came from a small town in southern Germany—there were another three siblings who pursued skilled trades in their hometown. At the big family dinner, the mother addresses her children. At last she comes to speak of both her dancer sons, sighs deeply with all motherly concern, and says, "*They haven't achieved anything.*".

> Whatever you personally think is a worthwhile goal—that's what we mean here when we talk about "success".

With the desire for success, artists start their way. The next step for many is to dedicate themselves to …

**Focus on the Market**
What is needed? How should I be? What is expected of me? What is currently successful? Where do I find a gap in the market for me? What seems like a sensible analysis at first can set off a chain reaction that turns self-marketing into an ordeal and pushes your career in a direction that doesn't suit you. You would notice this by wondering after years of hard work:

> "Why am I appreciated for something I don't like myself?"
> "Why did I give up at that point?"
> "Why don't I want to give what they want from me?"

To take up the terminology of the first chapter again: In this case, the *Third Person* would have dominated the second, the creative, and thus committed a crucial error. Because for your creative self this creates a …

**Distance from the Creative Core**

If creatives focus on the market and orient their artistic activities and self-marketing primarily on what is wanted there, they distance themselves from their most important capital—their creative core. From this substance—talent, personally relevant content and the will to express themselves—they have been feeding themselves since early childhood. The creative core accompanies artists throughout their lives and is as natural to them as the act of breathing. It is therefore not uncommon for them to underestimate its importance and fail to nurture it sufficiently. Most creatives I deal with say "I am sure of my artistic talent and ability, but the selling part is difficult for me". Therefore they do not protect this part sufficiently. I have already explained in the first chapter how dramatic it is for creative people when they become estranged from what they do. Artists do not make art because they have discovered a market niche that they now want to fill. They do what is already inside them—independent of fashions or zeitgeist. They can be more or less in tune with their era, which in turn has an influence on how well they can sell their art. At best, they set a trend themselves. If they allow their view of the market to dominate the creative core, they reinforce the belief that success is based on market analysis and satisfying the needs of that market. This is certainly a connection that has its justification in purely market-based contexts.

> For creatives there is no marketing without self and no self without art.

The basis of a successful self-marketing strategy is therefore the cultivation of the creative core. In the "Angelic Ladder of Self-Marketing" we devote ourselves in detail to the question of what is meant by the "creative core" and how it can be nurtured. Furthermore, there is another reason why focusing on the market makes little sense in the artistic field: It doesn't exist—*the* market! What Hubert Thurnhofer beautifully depicts with his "art market pyramid" for the visual arts also applies to all other arts: there are numerous different markets, which are also constantly in motion. What is a "no-go" today may already be the focus of interest tomorrow. In addition, artists today can create their own markets with the possibilities of self-promotion via the Internet. So those who chase the market are chasing a phantom, possibly causing fatal collateral damage in the process, because of…

**Reduced Access to Strengths**
If artists distance themselves from their creative core because they first focus their attention on the market and its supposed requirements, they inevitably distance themselves at the same time from their strengths, which are closely connected to this core. All of a sudden, the ingredients that normally feed their personality are missing: enthusiasm, openness, presence, individuality, energy, curiosity, expressiveness, charm, humor, body awareness, access to their own world of ideas and feelings. Visible to the outside and palpable to the inside, the message is: "You are not succeeding in convincingly promoting yourself." With this the…

**Insecurity Intensifies**
Creatives who lose the immediate proximity to their creative substance move like the penguin on land, because the feeling of alienation from oneself causes great insecurity. It seems as if one has forgotten why one's art is worth putting out there—let alone one's own person. Feelings of shame come to the fore and hinder the ability to communicate. The right words, the power of persuasion, the courage and

self-confidence to stand up for oneself and present one's own work and skills are lacking. This occurrence sets in motion a self-reinforcing destructive cycle that is so uncomfortable that the individual wants to escape it as quickly as possible. This need often manifests itself as …

**Withdrawal**

One retreats from the arena of self-marketing. This withdrawal can take the form of avoidance behaviour, but also defiance, arrogance, depressive moods or self-accusations. Artists and performers are also very inventive when it comes to self-sabotage strategies. The result is …

**Lack of Visibility**

They are too little or not visible at all on the market. In the literal sense: there is nothing to be seen of them. Channels on which interested parties would like to be informed remain undersupplied. Material is outdated or does not meet their needs. Networking meetings take place without them. Not only on the official stage: even in private circles, in conversation—even with confidants—the withdrawal becomes noticeable and this results in …

**Lack of Resonance**

The longed-for connection cannot take place. There is also no exchange that stimulates growth and new inventions. It is as if the mill wheel is at a standstill because there is no (more) water to drive it and that in turn …

**Increases the Desire for Success**

As the will to express continues because it exists independently of what is happening in the market, a haggard person is left behind who now asks himself even more longingly: "Where is my place?". Usually, there is reliance on the inner drive that ensures that creatives, after (sometimes very long) periods of invisibility, break out again to show themselves. It's also often friendships, fans or other support systems that can't stand to see the talent wither or go unnoticed that encourage them or offer help.

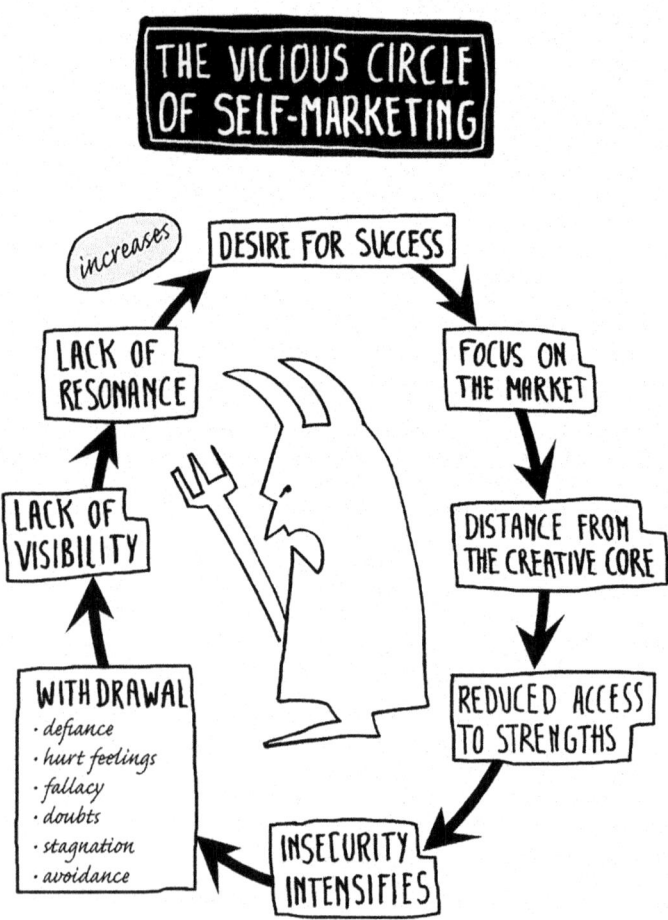

Vicious Circle of Self-Marketing

I do not want to assert a universal truth with the model of this vicious circle, but by exaggerating it I want to underline the fatal effect it can have on creative personalities if they do not sufficiently appreciate their most important resource—their creative inner life—and instead allow themselves to be seduced into adapting to market events.

> Approach it differently this time. With staying power. Focused on keeping it up for years privately, artistically and strategically, and always flexible to changing priorities.

As a guide to this, I present below my model of the "Angelic Ladder of Self-Marketing".

# The Angelic Ladder of Self-Marketing: Caring for the Creative Core Is the Key

Having devoted more time to the not-to-do in the "Vicious Circle of Self-Marketing," we are now heading straight for the start of your personal self-marketing. Just as the vicious circle is a self-reinforcing destructive cycle, the angelic ladder can set in motion a positive reinforcing cycle. It too begins with the …

**Desire for Success**

The original drive, your personal elixir, which was already mentioned in the first part of this book, is no different in both cycles. As already explained in Part I, it is important that you constantly reexamine what you personally understand by it. The definition of success changes with you. Immediately after your education, after a few years on the job, while starting a family or when the children have moved out, you assess the same situation quite differently.

> **What Is Success?**
>
> So if you're currently looking to revamp your self-marketing, take the time to think carefully about what you'd like to end up with:
>
> - What do you want your life to look like in 3–5 years?
> - How would you know you were getting closer to your version of success?

> - What could fill you with a deep sense of pride, gratitude, or joy?
> - If necessary, give concrete figures (monthly income, shooting days, picture prices, fees, etc.).
> - How would you be portrayed in the media when you are at the peak of your career?

The crucial difference between the vicious circle and the angelic ladder is that in the first step you do not turn to the market requirements, but to …

## Caring for the Creative Core

> Focus attention inward—not outward.

> **Caring for the Creative Core**
>
> Think about what the term "creative core" might mean for you personally. First of all, ask yourself what you understand by it:
>
> - Is it how you feel about yourself?
> - A state you're going into?
> - During which activities do you get into a flow experience, forget about time and feel refuelled and nourished afterwards?
> - Do you rather understand a certain aesthetic, an understanding of art with which you identify?
> - Is it a collection of adjectives, nouns and images that, taken together, would describe your creative core well?
>
> Then ask yourself:
>
> - What connects you to this core?
> - What brings your second person—your creative self—to life?

> - What helps you get into a creative state (e.g. quiet, being undisturbed, certain people, enough time, an inspiring space)?
> - What is stopping you (e.g. you haven't eaten properly, lack of materials, pressure, certain people, an expectation)?
> - How high does the dose of this substance have to be in order for the connection to your second person not to break off?
>
> If you're having a hard time answering these questions, try to remember what it was like for you as a child. How did you manage to turn on creative mode back then?

Whether creatives are in vital connection with their creative core is not always tied to the fact that they practice the art all the time. They are usually very good at telling you whether that connection is currently neglected or well cared for. I worked with a client whose goal was to finally make writing a vibrant part of their life. In the beginning, we had to literally wring concrete writing time out of her jam-packed daily life against great resistance. Bit by bit, we conquered a little more writing territory. Eventually it became a no-brainer. Once, as usual, when I asked at the beginning of our conversation how the writing was going, she said, "*I haven't put anything on paper in the last two weeks, but it's all fine—I'm in touch with the text internally.*"

The cultivation of the creative core should happen completely independently of what is happening in the market. Without a goal and without artistic compromise. It is dedicated solely to maintaining your creative source. Think of your creativity like a shy animal that can only show itself and get into the right mood under special circumstances. Treat it sensitively and with care. Neglect this little animal and you will have nothing to market yourself for. It can't be valuable enough to you. Defend it and protect it, and if it shows itself cautiously, do not immediately open the doors to streams of visitors. Initial ideas, first attempts and new directions are like tender little plants that should not be exposed to the weather yet. Nurture them well, and they will return the favor by appearing when you need them and provide you with confidence, flow of ideas, and self-assurance.

Surely you know this: When you are in contact with your creative core either through a job, an idea you are working on or an intensive practice phase—you experience the world and yourself in it differently. You remember who you (actually) are and what gives your life meaning. You feel stronger and more willing to take risks than during periods when you have not been creative for a long time. For some creatives, this aspect is so strong that by the morning after a premiere, they're already not quite sure if they're allowed to feel like they belong to the creative world. The connection to your second person is sensual in nature—it cannot be made solely through thought. Creative personalities need to experience this other state of consciousness in real terms in order to reassure themselves. This has a positive effect on your self-marketing in two ways. First:

**Products Emerge**
This automatically produces an artistic outcome. This does not necessarily mean products ready for publication such as DVDs, books or CDs. It can also be ideas, drafts, sketches, models, presentation material or similar. Secondly, it allows you …

**Access to Strengths**
The opposite of what happens in the vicious circle happens: you stay in touch with your strengths. The creative activity gives you access to character traits that are typical for people

who create art and are also wonderfully suited to inspire others for themselves. What you use on stage, in the rehearsal room, in the studio, while writing, in front of the camera or in the workshop is now available to you to promote yourself: your authentic enthusiasm, openness, presence, your individuality and energy, curiosity and expressiveness. The inner freedom to use your charm and humour. An unadulterated body awareness and access to your world of ideas and feelings. What proves useful in producing art, equally supports you in marketing yourself. This connection must not be severed when it comes to self-marketing strategies. It causes what we want to achieve: You get the…

**Desire to Show Yourself**
Most creatives claim that they are bad at "selling themselves". You can quickly illustrate that this is not true: Remember the last time you were in a creative flow state and a product came out of it. Were you desperate to withhold it from those around you afterwards? Or did you reveal some of it at the first good opportunity? As a rule, when you have created something out of yourself, you feel the desire to show it to the outside world. This desire arises from the creative product—the song, text, film, the project idea. Artists enjoy giving themselves away as a medium for this work. They only need to do what they love in order to enjoy and be enthusiastic about it and to transfer this joy and passion to others. That's why they are actually born advertisers. The prerequisite for you to access this talent is that you recognize the value of your product. It is you, your art, your creativity, your virtuosity, your humor, your understanding of language, your musicality, your stories that are at stake here. No one but yourself can create these products. Each artist produces for a specific market, their own fan base, target audience and followers what is welcome to

them. This market has to be found and made known with your own creative substance.

If you lack the drive to show up, you can ask yourself two questions:

1. Have I taken care of my product responsibly enough?
2. Am I in the right market?

This procedure leads to your ...

**Visibility**
When you nurture your creative substance, you hold products in your hand that you love to showcase. This automatically makes you visible. This doesn't have to be directly in the media. It can happen just by talking about what you're working on over dinner in private, or briefly hinting at something during production breaks, or questions arise and you contact someone about it, and they find out about what you're doing. Of course you also become visible on the market—on playbills, art fairs, in announcements, reviews, at premiere parties, flyers, on the radio, television, the Internet, at openings, panel discussions, festivals, resulting in ...

**Resonance**
You are noticed, people react to you. With this you achieve a ...

**Network Expansion**
What is particularly important here is that the closer you have stayed to your creative core along the way, the more fruitful the network expansion that results will be. This is because for you only a network that suits you, and what you have to offer, is interesting. More and more you will feel that where you offer your art, they are pleased that you do.

The less you will have the feeling that you are ingratiating yourself there.

On the one hand, the angelic ladder is for the efficient use of all resources to establish oneself. On the other hand, it can be helpful when actual circumstances are such that you have to be unfaithful. I'd like to explain why this doesn't contradict my passionate plea for creatives to stay as close to their artistic identity as possible: it's not uncommon for doors to open that don't have much to do with the artistic core, but pay the rent or seem strategic for other reasons. If creatives are in a tangibly living connection to their artistic identity, a necessary deviation from that path will cause them much less distress, because they won't confuse the job with their creative self. I know some who are commercially very successful in a market that tends to leave them personally cold, but have thus created the opportunity to realize their heart's projects. It would not be helpful to restrict artists too much in their working possibilities—it is much too difficult to support oneself exclusively through art. For me, it's about motivating them to use every opportunity to promote themselves. Precisely *because* it's so hard. In doing so, they should feel free to choose their paths and just not lose the connection to the starting point.

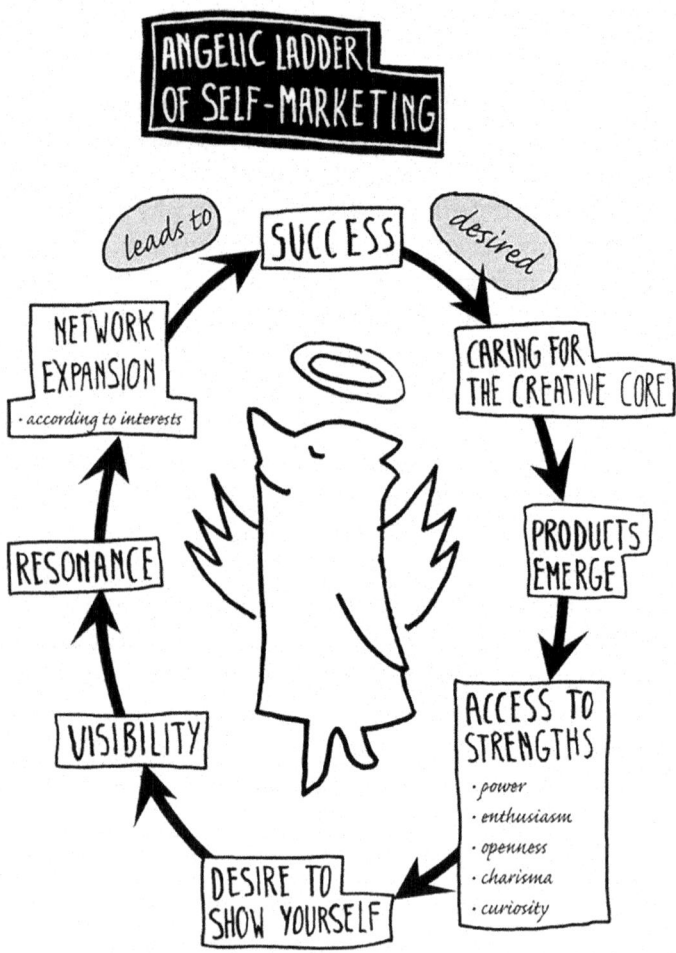

Angelic Ladder of Self-Marketing

Clarissa found herself in precisely this dichotomy: how should she deal with the fact that the market defines her in a way that doesn't suit her, but secures her existence?

## Clarissa, 26

*I am a petite woman with big blue eyes and a small nose. Apparently, this outer appearance causes that people like to put me in the drawer "cute mouse". If I follow this pigeonhole, many doors open for me, but not the ones I would like. I'm at a crossroads again right now: should I go for an offer that will feed me for a long time and give me some name recognition, but is too empty of content for my taste? Don't I then move further and further away from who I really am?*

## Alina Gause

Many years ago, I interviewed an actor on the subject of creatives caught between career and vocation, and she told me the following: *"At drama school, we all swore we'd never do soaps. We're never going to do that! Then I remember very clearly how we were all sitting in the dressing room—Dana, Bea and I—and then Bea said, 'They offered me this soap. Do you want me to do it, I don't know.' We're all like, 'Do it! Come on, a year of real grit, every day you're shooting and who knows what will come out of it!', and then she said: "It didn't work out." So we said: "Be happy! That would have been terrible! You don't know what kind of soap it is!' Then she came back the next day: 'They made a mistake, I'm in after all!' And we said: 'Great! Really good!' That's how it is, that's how you become."* Is that what you become? You blow with the wind with no real passions or convictions? Totally alienated by external dictates? It can happen. The gap between supply and demand is wider than in almost any other industry. Many artists therefore become the plaything of the job market and some end up looking back on a life that does not suit them. And yet they had set out to lead a particularly free life! A life that follows their longing for the expression of personally meaningful themes! What should one advise an actor, singer, musician, author or director today, to whom, like you, doors open that promise commercial success, but miss their inner calling? I would say: Walk through them, not everyone in this profession has that opportunity—but walk vigilantly. Take it one step at a time, asking yourself each time, *"Why am I doing this right now?"* Can you maybe use one for the other? Is it just fun? Are

> there other good reasons? What dose of *"I'm not quite me."* can you tolerate? This is where creative personalities differ significantly and often don't take their feelings seriously enough. It is the inner thread that must ultimately guide you through your question. Listen attentively within yourself and continue to work in parallel on what your heart really beats for. Then you can also sometimes take paths that seem artistically suspect to you. In order to be able to say, *"That wasn't mine, that's why I set the course differently,"* you also have to try it. That doesn't mean you're lost to "true" art—even if some guardians of truth would like to pin you down to it. It is a difficult task today, as it was in the past, to make an artist's life for yourself that nourishes your body, mind and soul well. Gourmets, frutarians, home cook lovers—there's everything on the market. Find out what diet you need to avoid stomach aches and stay sustainably healthy. Then, in retrospect, you won't have to agonize (*"Why didn't I …"*, *"Why did I only …"*), but can acknowledge the balance of career and vocation as a life achievement and say, *"It wasn't easy to survive in the profession and stay true to myself while doing it, but I managed it well."*

Finally, a note: Of course, there are concepts in the creative industry that are geared exclusively towards the market. These are products that are created on the drawing board and are invariably oriented towards what can achieve the highest sales figures. Based on this, the product is developed, the protagonists are then selected and "inserted" into the finished image. This is not to say that these concepts do not place any value on content, however content and artistic quality are only relevant in terms of sales figures—on their own they are meaningless. I've seen this up close and personal a few times with large media conglomerates. It's a viable path to entrepreneurial success, but not a way for a creative personality who has to master the sensitive balancing act between profession and vocation. I know the difficult situation in which artists find themselves when they are made an offer that promises them a platform that can hardly be achieved on their own. I have not yet experienced that this has led to a goal for them—at most for a short time. Conversely, I know creatives who have regretted this step all their lives.

Exciting artistic products are built on heart and soul, great emotions, an impressive willingness to perform and a high level of meaning for the creators. The marketing of this fragile, vibrant commodity follows different laws and my approach takes this into account. For everyone else, there is a wide range of reading based on other premises.

# The Quarter-Hour Policy: Finding Space and Time

We've talked about the right attitude, we've calibrated your compass to the best starting direction. Now let's get to work! For this you need three things:

1. Space
2. Time
3. Agenda

**Space**
You need a space for your creative person and a space for your *Third Person*. Whether these are two different spaces is one of the first decisions you will make. Think carefully about what criteria the two spaces need to meet. For performing artists, for example, it is important who can listen to them while they practice. What equipment do the spaces need? What about the financial resources? Do organisational circumstances determine the location?

Problems are sure to arise in the search for the right space. Do not be discouraged. When I first started out, I used to let people convince me that the problems were unsolvable. In the meantime, I know so many creative, successful solutions for workspaces—on a small budget and with a large family—that I am convinced that you too will find a solution. Two examples:

A pianist had two wonderful grand pianos in his large apartment—everything seemed perfect. Therefore, at first it was far from his mind to look for an additional space, also because he would not have been able to find the money for it. However, we realized that he felt unfree to practice for hours in his rented house and also to make mistakes. We put finding an undisturbed rehearsal space at the top of the priority list. It took some time, but eventually he found it in Waldorf schools and community centers.

Two artists swapped apartments for their office time. They were too distracted in their own private spaces. The necessary data could be easily transported via laptop and as useful side effects they told me that this way they had to keep to the times more bindingly and furthermore they enjoyed tidying up their workplace and making it particularly appealing for their colleague.

So look for solutions to your individual problems until you find your space or spaces. Design your working environment in such a way that it makes you want to work. Also expect that the people around you—partners, family, the apartment community or the neighbourhood—will not immediately pull in the same direction. Explain yourself. People working in the arts often feel they are not allowed to claim anything for themselves because they usually earn less (monetarily). As a result, they have a hard time legitimizing investment. Without investment—temporal, financial, mental, emotional—you can't do (self-)marketing. By finding a space, you take the first step in this direction.

## Time

Research, office work, applications, the production of presentation material—all this takes a lot of time. And so it can quickly happen that self-marketing seems like an impossibility. It seems like a mountain that causes exhaustion even before you climb it, just by looking at it. I counter this once again with the pleasure principle, on the one hand, and the policy of small steps, on the other. Creatives often don't know how many time-eaters there are in their lives. They lurk everywhere, but disappear just as quickly as they arose when an endeavor that really captivates them comes along. Then they suddenly discover units of time that they wouldn't have recognized as such in the past. However, this sometimes results in them losing sight of their strength, working to exhaustion and then looking all the more disillusioned at the mountain that remains. Therefore, your *Third Person* should combine the benefits of the pleasure principle with the benefits of continuous, small steps.

> Find your model of time and day structuring.

We know from educational psychology that people differ in how they work best. Some love music or sitting in the hustle and bustle of a café, others need silence. For some it helps to know that their time is limited, others need an open end. Schools have been trying for some time to integrate this knowledge into the way they teach and to accommodate different temperaments, speeds and types of learners. The structures of the institutions set certain limits to these efforts. You, on the other hand, are allowed to shape your work environment to your own taste—take advantage of it! What is your preferred mode? If you don't know yet, find out now.

**My Work Mode**

1. Time unit
   Define clear and realistic work units for yourself. Try out different models. What about your concentration? Are you more of a long or short distance type? Which task fits best with the unit of time you have at the moment?
2. Time of day
   Find out at what time of day you can muster the most suitable energy for which activity. Proofreading a text, doing the tax return, researching agencies, making phone calls, composing a song, developing a vision—each action requires different resources.
3. Breaks
   Schedule breaks, remember to eat and drink enough. One or the other may laugh at this, but food intake is a frequent topic in my consultations—both for those who eat too little and for those who eat too much. The flow state that the second person, your creative self, gets into numbs not only the sense of time, but also other physical sensations such as hunger, thirst, or pain. Taking timely breaks, eating balanced meals and drinking enough fluids will make you work more efficiently.
4. After work…
   Observe how your work sessions affect you the following day. You may have spent a lot of time researching and not realize until it's far too late that your battery is completely drained, making it that much harder to get things done the next day. Also reward yourself for doing a good job.

I myself experienced the combination of the pleasure principle and the policy of small steps as the strategy of choice when I was studying psychology, caring for two children and also writing and staging solo musical theatre shows. It was in the combination of these different activities that I personally found the appeal and thus the drive. I was often asked, "How do you do it? So much at once!". I could have basked in that recognition, but I knew better and thought, "If you only knew—Take away one of the pillars and I'd lose interest immediately." In the combination of family, art and science I felt I was best represented as a total personality and had found the appropriate powerhouse for me. One area less and I would have had to expend a lot more energy to achieve the same thing (and probably would have left it). However, I admittedly had to be efficient with the limited time I had. So, for me, I invented the "Quarter-Hour Policy." That is, any unit that provided at least 15 undisturbed minutes for me, I recognized and used as a meaningful unit of work.

> Make self-marketing a part of your daily life.

# Office Time: Your Essential Tool for Climbing the Mountain

All tasks around the topic of self-marketing should take a manageable but reliable part in your life from now on. For this I would like to give you my concept of "Office Time" as a guide for the policy of small steps. In the "Office Time", all *Third Person*-tasks are done.

**Time Limit** For those who do not currently have any fixed appointments, I recommend a time limit: at least 1 h, at most 2 per day. At least 5 days, at most 6 per week. That is, 1 day a week should be free of all obligations. For those who already have a jam-packed schedule, I advise finding small but mandatory additional time units. The time limit here is to be taken very seriously: do not underestimate the effort that dealing with *Third Person*-tasks will cost you—mental effort. You should only allow yourself to do this in manageable doses.

**General Conditions** Treat this time as seriously as you would a job or engagement. There you would not look at your cell phone, not eat, not be disturbed by private phone calls. Defend this time in your social environment as well—to your family, to your partner, to your circle of friends or to your shared apartment.

**Agenda** After the question of space and time, it is now about your agenda. Below you will find the contents that you will work on in your "Office Time" and thus the tasks that your *Third Person will* take over:

- Create and work through to-do lists (and if necessary not-to-do lists)
- Create short-, medium- and long-term schedules
- Research of offers, applications, cooperations, market events
- Private and professional bureaucracy
- PR-material creation and maintenance
- Network expansion and maintenance
- Professional phone calls and mails
- Regularly balance your artistic, private and economic books
- Social media
- Development and implementation of own marketing ideas
- Keeping an eye on and coordinating the tasks of all three personality parts

I deliberately chose the term "Office Time" to make it clear that you can't expect fun and fulfillment there. This relieves you of the unrealistic obligation to be enthusiastic about *Third Person*-tasks. Nevertheless, I would encourage you to follow the pleasure principle with your to-do lists as well: which of the tasks on the agenda triggers the least resistance in you at this moment?

The "Office Time" follows the policy of small, continuous steps. It deals leniently and lovingly with the creative soul and yet firmly with any inner resistance. Try it out: already in the first month you will be surprised what you have achieved, what you have shied away from in the months before.

# OFFICE TIME

## TIME LIMIT
- 5-6 days per week
- 1-2 hours per day

## GENERAL CONDITIONS
- no disturbances
- represented to the outside as working time
- does not have to be pleasant
- do not question

## TASKS
- to-do list
- research
- schedules
- distribute tasks to 1st, 2nd and 3rd person
- private bureaucracy
- professional mails, phone calls
- material refreshing, PR...

Office Time

# The Work Wish List: Networking According to Your Taste

Sometimes I ask my counterpart to draw up a "Work Wish List". This might include colleagues as well as artistic directors, musical directors, roles, shows, institutions, theatres, companies. Personally known to us or unknown, either currently or formerly. There may be names on it, of which it is unlikely that a cooperation will come about—this list is compiled without a reality check. You may list people on there that you wouldn't even know how to get the contact details of at the moment. People whose names you don't know or no longer remember, who you met in a production, during your studies or training, or in a workshop, and for whom you regret that you did not maintain contact. Two criteria should be decisive for whether the person or institution is listed there:

- A:
  You have an honest interest in the person or institution that is not based solely on their success.
- B:
  You expect growth—personal, commercial, artistic—from this contact. Hang this list in a place you walk by every day, such as the refrigerator, and keep adding to it contacts that are close to your heart, with whom you identify, feel comfortable with, and in your element, or believe would be so in a collaboration. This has two main functions:

1. On the list is the description of your personal habitat.

    It creates an image of the environment in which you would feel like a penguin in the water and relieves you of the feeling of obligation to perform at your best even in the desert. We know it's hard to achieve working in the conditions you dream of, but that's easier to deal with than the feeling of being a failure.

2. You should have this list at hand when you need it.

    This is when you are ready for new marketing actions. For example, because now you have new material or new projects, or because you want to improve your job opportunities, or simply because now you have the time. If you try to create such a list spontaneously, it's like restaurants—you can't think of any that you really wanted to try out and now have the opportunity to do so. That's why the list should be enriched bit by bit—every time someone comes to your mind. If the moment has come when you need them, you look at the list and perhaps discover—again following the pleasure principle—a name with which you now have the motivation and courage to make contact. You leave all the others to one side until a new moment comes.

> **Three Goals and Three Deadlines**
>
> To conclude this second part, I would like you to formulate and write down three specific marketing plans. Possible examples would be:
>
> - Make a professionally important contact;
> - Create presentation material (press releases, flyers, business cards, photos, videos, audio demos, project sketches, a scaled design model);
> - Use a promotional platform (such as a trade show, social media or other networks on the Internet, print media, a networking meeting);
> - Invest in technical equipment or
> - Research.

> Set a deadline for each of these goals.
> Think of each implementation like a research trip that will provide you with important information for future marketing campaigns:
>
> - What comes easy to you? What do you find difficult?
> - Where do you discover similarities with the perspective I represent here and where does it differ from yours?
> - Are you experiencing any surprises?
> - Who can answer your open questions?
> - At what point would support be helpful?
> - What can you do yourself?
>
> At the end, take stock of where you see opportunities for improvement.

Whether the effort and return on an investment are in good proportion to each other can sometimes only be judged after years, because self-marketing does not lead from A to B. Sometimes you've already reached Q and all of a sudden B happens as a sequence of activities that were initially seemingly unrelated. For example, you're at an art opening or a film festival reception and you were "just" talking in a group about horses or vintage cars or Chinese medicine or your kids. In hindsight, you think the evening would have been just as meaningful on the sofa at home. Months later, that very information (he can ride or she has access to a large indoor arena where classic cars are) may be of interest to you, or you might meet someone from that group again at the next networking meeting and feel a little more comfortable right away. It is one of the most common misconceptions that artists expect promotional activities to produce directly noticeable effects. That may be so, but it doesn't have to be. I asked a performer, who I knew invested a lot and acted successfully for herself in a round of artists, if she would reveal what principle she acted on. Her answer, "*The more I throw at the wall, the more I end up with.*"

# Part III

## Be Visible

I can understand that it is enormously difficult for non-artistic practitioners to believe when those in the arts—especially the performing arts—find encounters with the public a burden. Posing on the red carpet, putting yourself out there in an interview, or giving the public (sometimes daily) a personal glimpse. To the environment, it seems like a paradox: "For years you've been trying to get public attention. Finally everyone is noticing you and suddenly you don't want it? What's wrong with you?" Psychologically, this apparent contradiction is rather a proof that everything is right, because the exposed position in artistic professions is only partially compatible with the needs of a healthy person. We experience this particularly when people achieve a high level of prominence and are therefore very exposed. This challenging effect is intensified when this happens at a young age, when personality development is still in its adolescence.

> Being the focus of attention, especially intense, with few time-outs, out of one's own control, is a great psychological challenge. This is true for all people—including creative people.

It is commonly assumed that artists are different from the average population in this respect. This is a misconception that unfortunately persists and means that they are often alone when too much publicity overwhelms them. The greatest disappointment they direct at this is against themselves, as they usually expect themselves to be up to it. Moreover, their environment reacts without understanding. Most people think that people with an artistic streak are extraverted, exhibitionistic and narcissistically inclined personalities who love to reveal themselves as limitlessly as possible at all times. No. They aren't. In fact, the opposite is often true. In the case of commercially very successful artists, the situation is sometimes aggravated by the fact that a large part of the family and circle of friends is existentially dependent on this "business", and the celebrity is under pressure not only from his or her own existence, but also from that of the most important people to whom he or she relates.

A particularly tragic example of the lack of understanding with which the environment can react to the excessive demands of an artist can be seen in the documentary "Avicii—True Stories". It tells the story of DJ Avicii's breakdown, which supposedly leads to a happy ending: he pauses and treats himself to some much-needed time off. The film ends here. Shortly after a streaming service released the documentary, it was revealed that Avicii died under mysterious circumstances. The family had alluded that he had committed suicide. Now, one always has to be skeptical of biographical content that is exclusively available through the media. In this case, however, we witness in the documentary "live", so to speak, how Avicii repeatedly emphasizes that it has become unbearable for him to show himself to the public, thus eliciting only incredulous waving from those present. The fact that he completes a concert in front of countless people a few minutes after his desperate statement serves as proof to those involved that his complaint cannot possibly be true. It is interpreted as temporary stage fright. A fatal error.

For many artists, finding a healthy way to deal with the tensions of living in the public eye remains a challenge throughout their lives. Often they use art as an outlet to overcome introversion, shyness or closed-mindedness and still be able to communicate through the channel of artistic expression. Perhaps the inner life is like a volcano that would not be easily expressed in a socially conforming everyday life. It's a bit like Goethe's "The ghosts I called…": artists want their product to be devoured, but as a person they want to experience it from a safe distance. The proximity of product and person makes it difficult to keep a distance, which makes it all the more important to take strategic precautions here. This is another benefit of the concept of the first, second and *Third Person*: it can be determined more precisely which part of the personality likes to be in the centre of attention and whether the other two can follow. If one does not address these questions in a differentiated manner, one may wonder for the rest of one's life why the applause at the end of a performance or concert is one of the most unbearable moments of the profession, as is often reported.

## Interim Audit Before the Final Spurt

In the first step you have found a supportive basic attitude and in the second step you have already come into practical action. You are now well equipped for the third step—being visible:

1. You consider yourself and your art a treasure to be cherished.
2. You'll forgive yourself if self-marketing doesn't come easily to you, but requires strategic thinking and a disciplined approach.

3. You look at your life as an artist like you look at a business that needs a team to succeed.
4. You allow yourself to proceed according to the pleasure principle: that is, in everything that has to be done, you look for the aspect that most excites you and start there.
5. You have created an undisturbed working space—for artistic activity and office time.
6. You have equipped these rooms with the necessary materials.
7. You have a schedule with work units to which you have assigned different task areas.
8. You have created an agenda with short-, medium- and long-term tasks.
9. Throughout all of this, you remain a creative personality and are always ready to shape plans and tasks in a flexible, individual and imaginative way.

On this foundation, the chances are good that you will actually do what comes next and for a long time. We turn in the following to the concrete marketing aspects that one had possibly already expected at the beginning of the book:

- How do you become part of your business and what does that mean to you?
- Which presentation material should you create, which is not necessary?
- How do you represent your contractual claims?
- What support would you like to add to your inner team of first, second and *Third Person*?

# Life in Business: Who's Who and Who Does What, and Why You Should Know

The artistic profession has offered me many opportunities to wonder. About casts, about fashions, about communication styles, about successes and failures. Much seems unpredictable, opaque, unfair, even cruel. However there is one aspect that makes me think that this elusive business also knows justice:

> Those who invest the most usually get the furthest.

I became aware that I now hold this conviction when, in an interview, I answered the question, "What is it about some that makes them more successful than others?" not by shrugging my shoulders as I usually do, but by saying, "The amount of input, the stamina, and the nurturing of creative substance." It sounds simplistic, but it's not. It will always be a fascinating mystery of great careers, how they came to be. Where does someone get the strength? How are ideas born? Powerful creative relationships? What makes someone get up at 4:30 a.m. every day and work hard until midnight? What makes people take high financial and personal risks? Why does someone manage to overcome deep fears?

I make two assertions:

1. Creatives are doubly rewarded for their efforts—by personal satisfaction and increasing external success.
2. If either fails to materialize for years with high input, it's time for a thorough review.

Those who love their genre and acquire full expertise in it will be loved back. Filmmakers should love to see films and therefore know who is working on what and why. They should attend a festival because they can meet people and see films that interest them, not because they are aiming to get a job. Decision makers, employees, employers in the creative industries quickly recognise who is dedicated to the cause, just like they are, and who has only come for a short visit. Dedication, passion and above average effort are expected but also rewarded. In doing so, those who make a selection also legitimize and acknowledge their own effort. So if someone comes along and says: "I sing pop, but I also think opera is quite fun and I'd like to sing Carmen for you now," it's not looked upon so favourably—even if the singer could manage it vocally. On the one hand, this attitude leads to mistakes, such as when musical theatre performers are not acknowledged as being able to act. Likewise when exciting talents don't meet the criteria of predetermined pigeonholes, are perhaps ahead of their time, and thus don't meet existing ideals. On the other hand, what it means for you is that by clearly delineating and populating your habitat, you can focus your investments and maximize your chances of success. So become part of your profession!

> **Exercise Industry Knowledge**
>
> What exactly is your profession? In order to be able to enliven it according to your personal, authentic interest, you must first find out.

> Ask yourself:
> - What are the major industry events?
> - How well do you know the related trades and institutions of your art form (stage design, camera, sound engineering, graphics, photography, further education institutes, …)?
> - Do you know which professional associations, collecting societies, unions and insurers can be useful for you or where you can get information about them?
> - Are you familiar with the current trends and developments in your genre?
> - What about professional politics—do you know your rights and obligations?
> - Do you know in which media the latest information for your industry can be found?
> - Do you have a personal viewpoint on this?
> - Do you articulate this view—publicly or not, on a large or small scale?
> - Do you know about important awards, scholarships, funding opportunities in your industry?
>
> Thoughts and research like these should fill your "Office Time" in the future. Align these overarching questions with your specific subject. Consider the practical study of them like an additional study, where you give yourself the stamps for the courses you have completed. Also create documents on all questions and update them from time to time.

If, during this exercise, a mountain seems to be piling up which you are already exhaustedly shying away from climbing, reconsider the policy of small steps: take on a clearly defined, small part for each office time and deepen your knowledge a little bit more. As a rule, only the entry into a new, perhaps unloved subject area is difficult—you have chosen your profession because you are burning for it, this feeling will take over again after an initial phase of "strangeness".

It's not about carrying all this around like a burden: "Another new article I haven't read." "There's this event tonight. What am I going to do there? But I have to go!". That would go against everything I've advocated so far. This is about the fine line of why you choose not to subscribe to an industry magazine, take a continuing education course, or attend an event. Do you do it because you have enough information and experience to assess what is useful or necessary, or because you want to avoid the challenge? Over the course of your professional life, develop your personal position on your profession and then translate it into concrete action. Do you want to remain apolitical because that suits you? Then don't comment on political issues. Learn about industry events locally, form an opinion about them, and choose what you want to attend in the future. Create your own personal life in your business.

> The important thing is not that you do everything and are everywhere, but that you know your stuff and make conscious decisions.

Many artists fear precisely this part of their professional life and thus deprive themselves of important resources because they avoid, for example, networking meetings or discussions. You can also put it this way: if you want to be successful in a profession, you must not flee from it. Therefore, the sooner you consciously look for the jobs that trigger this flight reflex the least, the better.

# Excursus: Not Me!—What #metoo Has to Do with Self-Marketing

Living in the artistic business today also means dealing with #metoo. This applies to everyone involved in the creative industry. At the height of the debate, I was repeatedly asked as a psychological expert to classify the reports and events concerning Harvey Weinstein, Kevin Spacey or the german director Dieter Wedel, for example. Unfortunately, the interest tended to relate to striking reports of experiences, the confirmation of existing clichés or simplified positions. This gave me the desire to express myself in a more differentiated way and, above all, to offer possible solutions. I did my own research and interviewed representatives of various professions in the artistic field about their experiences and attitudes. Among them were employees from the areas of directing, casting, editing, training, production as well as performers. In the following, I would like to elaborate on the insights I gained into what promotes the breeding ground for sexual assault and abuse of power in the artistic profession and how we could change this.

This book deals with the question of how creative personalities can offer themselves and their art without developing a feeling of ingratiation in the process. The difference between the two is the degree of dignity. Dignity is also at stake when behavior is inappropriate, assaultive, or hurtful, or when a compliment doesn't deserve that label. It is no coincidence that artists sometimes use the term "prostitution" to illustrate how difficult it is for them to advertise themselves. This is because in order to do so, they have to leave their protective space, show themselves and thus also surrender part of their control and hand themselves over. The product of artists consists to a large extent of personal, one could say intimate content that belongs in responsible hands. If there is a dignified space for this, impressive, touching top performances emerge. Creatives go deep inside themselves and thus convey insights and experiences to the audience, the readership, the art lovers, that go beyond what they can experience in their everyday lives or at all. What creatives make available of themselves is rarely accessible in real life. That's a central reason why we love art. This is why I advocate being especially careful to protect performers so as not to jeopardize these extraordinary insights. There are many artistic work contexts in which this succeeds. However, the creative business also provides a "good" breeding ground for irresponsible handling of this vulnerability. A book that deals with self-marketing in the creative industry cannot omit this topic. This is because one of the reasons why artists sometimes find it so difficult to promote themselves is that many have already experienced or observed professional abuse of power.

> Self-marketing and #metoo are directly related in that it is typically in situations of self-marketing that assault happens.

Even if you have not yet come into contact with the topic, #metoo has an impact on your self-marketing. It stimulates the discussion about how we want to treat each other and this can influence working conditions in the creative profession. A pleasant, safe working atmosphere encourages you to "step into the arena". Then we are allowed to be more sensitive and the process and the work are enhanced.

## #metoo

The hashtag #metoo paved the way in a special way for a new seriousness in dealing with sexualised violence and abuse of power in the artistic profession. It reduced the countless shades of transgressions to two syllables. Those affected, who had previously shied away from speaking out because they could not classify whether what they had experienced was relevant to the public, their environment or a court, were given a platform to confess without having to make that final decision. The number of people affected skyrocketed for all to see, and many who had previously believed they had no cause of their own to deal with the issue were forced to rethink. The extent of the spread through #metoo strengthened the backs of those who triggered a media avalanche with the publication of their story. In the prominent cases, it meant another wave of attacks for those affected. In addition to defamation lawsuits and professional damage, public opinion did not hold back either:

> "Why are they all coming up with this now? After all these years?"
> "They're just trying to do damage out of frustration at their own lack of success."
> "No sense of humor."
> "Aren't you even allowed to give compliments now?"
> "Why would he need to do that?"
> "Slept their way to the top. You know how it is."

#metoo challenges everyone involved in the profession to take a stand. Inspired by my own research, I remembered that I had encountered the unwritten laws long before I entered the profession:

I was 16—performing arts class in high school. Our teacher was gleefully rolling around on top of a classmate while touching whatever he felt like on her. We all laughed at his embarrassment—she did too. The course was over for her, though—the rest of us stayed.

I was 18, had just passed the entrance exam to drama school and was sitting in the café opposite a director who asked me to stand up and spin around a few times. He decided he wanted to take me to Denmark for his filming. I would just have to share a hotel room with him. I was disgusted, telling my girlfriends about it like it was a suspenseful horror movie. We agreed on who was to be judged and how. Nevertheless, I saved this encounter under the label "This is how a meeting with a director is."

I was 20—in acting training, the acting teacher took us through the warm-up: "*Breathe in through your asshole. Especially the females among you—blow your tits open—free yourselves.*" I breathed dutifully, suppressing the urge to vomit. I interpreted the discomfort at his "wording" as an obvious sign of my bourgeois uptightness.

I could go on like this forever. About myself, about others. Unpleasant but harmless stuff. Misguided compliments, and worse. Up to and including felonies, some reported, none punished, but that's not the point. My purpose in this excursus is threefold:

1. To create awareness of the breeding ground that fosters assault in the artistic field.
2. Identify steps needed to better control this breeding ground.
3. To inform. Especially for the less experienced among you, I would like to convey that you can trust your feelings: what feels wrong will most likely be wrong.

First of all, it should be noted once again: sexual assault has nothing to do with eroticism, love play, flirtation or an interesting tension between two people, but with power. One person does something that another person does not want, who either allows it because he/she otherwise has to fear a disadvantage from the power structure or dependency relationship or fends it off—with just this effect.

**The Breeding Ground**
As participants in the artistic market, you are in a relationship of dependency and this makes you particularly vulnerable to transgressions and abuse of power. This is true in any area of life where access to resources is hard to come by. Industry events would feel different to you in seconds if your job title on the name tag signaled decision-making power. If only the job titles were switched at the event, the people would be the same, but their roles would be different and so would the power structure in which you meet and act.

> Realize that the hierarchical structure of your business has long been decided by the time you get there.

If one day the number of artists falls far below the needs of the cultural institutions and the public, we will be presented with a completely different picture. I, at least, will not live to see those times. Your task, therefore, is rather to deal strategically and self-carefully with the prevailing relationship between supply and demand. Again, the better informed and prepared you are, the more (self-)aware you will be to deal with difficult self-marketing situations.

There are four aspects that favour the breeding ground for transgressions and abuse of power in the artistic profession and also make it more difficult to resist:

1. **The fewer common rules and values are agreed upon, the more likely people are to resort to socially undesirable behavior.**

The artistic profession prides itself on its unconventional approach to rules and boundaries. Where this begins, where it ends, when it makes sense and when it is harmful, this fine analysis is only devoted to sporadically and intuitively. I asked a person concerned whether it would have helped her if she had been informed in good time about what is customary and what is not. For example, that it is not customary to have to undress at an agency, as she was asked to do. She wasn't sure because she still might have thought, *"Well, it's not customary, but it seems to be here. This agency is special. If I want this, I have to do this."*

2. **The higher the pressure, the more willing people are to throw agreed rules and values overboard.**

   Artists are under a lot of pressure for a number of reasons:

   (a) The labour market is particularly tight.
   (b) This increases the dependency relationships and that in turn increases the pressure.
   (c) The identification with and longing for work is particularly high. Not playing is like the feeling of not really living. Conversely, playing conveys a feeling of liveliness. Private person and professional person merge more easily than in other professions.
   (d) Artists are constantly in an application situation.

3. **People act in such a way that it promises them a personal benefit.**

   Let's look at it soberly: power and sexual attractiveness are to be understood in the creative metier as effective means of payment in order to achieve a personal benefit. This may not be noble, but it is human. However, when they become the only currency between two people, the risk of assault increases. It should be remembered, however, that in a business deal, both parties are entitled to solicit and negotiate—yet the deal is only concluded when both parties have consented in full consciousness and of their own free will.

4. **For artists, access to psychological self-defence mechanisms is more difficult during work.**

    I call it the "Achilles Heel of the Artist" (for those interested, I go into this in detail in my book "Kompass für Künstler"): Creatives need to keep themselves emotionally receptive and permeable to their work. Building up psychological shields comes at the expense of their ability to express themselves. Escape, rebellion, denial—reactions that provide a protective function in many other professions—mean limiting their work material.

This last aspect is impressively described by a female performer who had resisted the offensive advances of a director and subsequently suffered through months of humiliating film work with him. She rightly expected a great deal of attention from the production and was therefore under great pressure to perform well. This pressure to perform well, i.e. to be open and permeable in her acting, made it difficult for her to distance herself internally or externally from the director's attacks during the shoot: *"The moment someone behind the camera says "Hmm, just not enough coming," I would always chalk it up to me as an artist. Would I always feel bad and couldn't push that away. The bad thing, of course, is you always blame yourself, because even while he was going off at me, I knew him to be a good director who was great with the other cast members and could recognize quality. Then, of course, the door is opened and you are totally at their mercy. Everyone in the team said to me at the time, "It's clear what's going on here, now don't take it to heart like that." But that's not possible. And when he then recognizes your little tension and says "Nothing. Sorry, there's nothing there." then of course you believe it. Everyone hung on his every word like sheep."*

It cannot be repeated often enough: artistic work requires a special protective space. If this protection is available, the personal commitment is experienced as fulfilling. If there is no protection, we have to do without. A very experienced and successful actor described this case that happened to her: "*A director who was already over 50 let me continue to improvise a phone sex scene for an eternally long time: he simply didn't say 'cut' or 'thank you' for minutes. The gentlemen on the team were rolling with laughter at the fat old lady faking a sex act. I've rarely felt so humiliated in my life, but my Prussian work ethic just wouldn't allow me to cut the scene. I did complain to the production manager afterwards, but of course that didn't make up for the overwhelming feelings of shame in the situation in question.*" As a rule, professionally active artists and performers overcome their defensiveness or shame and meet the outside demands. They see it as part of their job. Where this supposed professionalism leads, I will illustrate below with an example. In the long run, these impositions are not without consequences. They fill the inner vessel of grievances and the environment wonders when costume rehearsals, laughter or supposedly unimportant remarks ("Now loosen up." "Sexy, your outfit." "Can you do it with a little more sensuality?") turn out to be minefields.

The example: A drama student sought to talk to me—she reported her case to different contact points and allowed me to quote from the letter: "*In my third semester of drama school … At the age of 22, I was accepted into the agency … … At the beginning of the year 2017, Mr. … invited me … To a hotel …. When I met him there, he said he only met with those members of his agency who showed particular commitment and in whom he saw particular potential. … He said that it was important to him to be able to guarantee that when he received requests for artists from his agency, they would be willing and able to commit to permissive casting situations and shooting days. So he wanted to convince himself of this motivation and my commitment and thus put me under pressure to undress in his hotel room and in his presence. At first I avoided this request by changing the subject, but then he became more energetic and asked more directly, while he assured me that I was allegedly not a woman of his taste and age, because I was too young for him, which is why the inhibition threshold would be easier to break through. ... He himself sat on a chair and told me to undress in front of the mirror. I complied with this last request after racking my brains, as I was under extreme pressure to prove myself at that moment, since he assured me that he would otherwise never let me be cast for meaningful roles, but only for extra engagements. Standing in front of the mirror in my underwear, already exceeding my own personal limits, I asked him if this was enough, but he wanted to see me completely naked to test how brave I was. He commented on me saying, "You don't have much bust and butt, but the overall picture fits." I subsequently removed my underwear as well, then he walked up to me, stood behind me on the left and placed his left hand on my breast and asked me, ".... Now look in the mirror and tell me what you see and what you like about the person in the reflection (me)." ... He kept his hand on my chest the whole time. After my answer, he took his hand away and I put my clothes right back on very quickly. ... He would not let me go and as a result I had to more forcefully point out my time constraints in order to escape this situation and conversation without escalation. ... I have not been able to talk about this incident to anyone until recently because I was afraid to confide in anyone and be judged."*

After she sought me out, I asked three other women who I knew were or had been involved with this agent about their experiences of him and got the following answers:

"I can confirm absolutely nothing you wrote. I honestly wonder who would spread such nonsense around either."

"A resounding no from me. Anything else would be slander, and a woman has to be careful there, too."

"I had heard rumours about him inviting his female clients to the hotel for "camera workshops". I myself was not involved. ... It was always very much about the issue of nudity on camera. In general he behaved very unprofessionally, which I didn't want to admit for a long time. I'm glad I left the agency."

I had not doubted the authenticity of the statement of the drama student, yet the question arose for me: Is that enough to pursue the matter, if the statements diverge so much? After all, all are adults, can freely decide where to get rid of their clothes.

Weeks later, it happened to turn out in the course of my ongoing research: for more than a year before the young woman's statement to me, there had been another complaint about this matter to the association of agencies. I contacted her and learned of other female colleagues who were being pressured by the agent in question to take their clothes off via Skype or in a hotel room. He makes films of it and calls it "acting coaching". He asks about the size of the genitals. I am not aware of any of those I interviewed being put forward for a role as a result of the "nude casting". Over the next 3 years, I encountered a total of eight sufferers who independently described similar processes in great detail. I invited the women to exchange their experiences in my rooms, moderated by me. For some of the women concerned, this was a big step and it took some trust work for this meeting to take place. They agreed that their goal was to stop the agent, but that they did not want to press charges against him. We decided to turn to the existing contact points—for a legal classification and advice on what steps were available. The women had to give detailed verbal and written information about the incidents, sometimes several times, and were happy to do so in the belief that they could make a difference. However, when I asked three times, each time 6 months apart, what the state of affairs was, I was told each time that (for some reasons I could understand but for others that I really could not) nothing had happened. There was no news from the contact points, some of those affected had meanwhile withdrawn from the profession, others were now in the public eye and did not want to be associated with it (anymore). So while it seemed as if the matter had come to a standstill, I kept hearing about new assaults in the agency through my counseling work. I realized that even in this case, one day it might be, "Why are they coming up with this now?". My conclusion was that in the summer of 2020, I sought out a conversation with SPIEGEL writer Laura Backes. After another period of trust work, three women agreed to talk to her. Her article appeared ("The Fear is Greater," (Die Angst ist größer) No. 4/23.1.21) and, contrary to my rather low expectations, it brought long-overdue movement to the case: it was passed from woman to woman within the agency in question. More and more of those affected openly exchanged information with each other, got together and, according to my latest information, some are now also considering taking legal action against the agent. I was particularly pleased when two of the women who had called the accusations groundless at the beginning now thanked me for the initiative. Only through this had it been possible for them to recognize the abusive structures to which they had exposed themselves. The process of coming to terms with the situation had begun.

An assault happens quickly. The path afterwards can take decades. This is not least due to the fact that, according to the general view, the topic only concerns those who are directly involved. The view that only they can tell something about it, because only they are involved. Affected. Informed. Damaged. Guilty. Naive. Poor. Power-hungry and success-hungry. Weak characters. Badly brought up. Disturbed. Unsuccessful. Successful. Untalented. Brilliant. Deceitful. Calculating. Everyone else employed on set, in the theatre, in the studio, in publishing, in the university …? Not a chance. "*I'm not affected.*" Or as in the case of my inquiries:

> "I'm afraid I don't have anything to say about that."
> "*On the matter of … I don't have anything to say because I don't really know about it and I wasn't directly affected.*"

Not concerned. Nothing to say. Part of the system? Not me. I think this is wrong, and I agree with essayist and activist Rebecca Solnit, who said this about violence against women, "*We always think some are affected because they are raped, beaten, murdered, and others are spared. But what happens to other women happens to me.*" (The Daily Mirror (Der Tagesspiegel), August 30, 2020, p. 81). Her statement can be congruently applied to all those affected by assaults and abuse of power—regardless of gender, industry and extent of the incidents.

> What happens to your colleagues happens to you.

It is not by chance that I have called my remarks on this subject "excursus", because at first glance it goes far beyond the aspect of self-marketing. At second glance, however, it becomes clear: as long as an actor has to fear finding herself or himself in such a situation when applying to an agency (it is not the only agency from which such an approach has been reported), it will be difficult to regard self-marketing like a professional responsibility and not think oneself close to the muckraking corner in the process. How is it possible that only one of the people I interviewed about the agent in question thought the reports were even possible? Does this belong in a realm from which "reputable" people distance themselves? Is there a general belief that everyone has it in their own hands to prevent such situations?

When we humans are confronted with a disturbing fact which challenges us personally, we try to find explanations. This gives us orientation and orientation gives us support. We assemble the explanation from the knowledge available to us. This knowledge is usually incomplete, especially in the case of highly complex problems. This saddens some people more than others. And drives some more than others to really get to the bottom of it. To admit new information that could shake one's own set of values, one's own convictions and thus one's familiar self-image. For this reason, paradigm shifts ("The earth is a disc." → "The earth is round.") are a very slow process of ever-new insights that must continually shake us and become more and more familiar until they can replace the old beliefs. Each shaking carries the potential to trigger a change. Whether it happens depends on whether enough people agree that it will benefit them. The sexism debate, the #metoo solidarity, the replacing of Kevin Spacey will all spur consequences when a majority expect to reap personal benefits. Christine Knauff, director of STARTER—Schauspielschule für Film und Fernsehen in Berlin, told me in an interview I did with her on the subject: *"Our industry ... which is supposed to move, touch, shake up, make you think or simply entertain— would do well, in my opinion, if it didn't just check production conditions for criminally relevant behaviour, but also faced up to the discussion on an everyday basis about how we treat each other, what kind of climate we want. ... Not (just) so that we all have a good time, no: so that we produce even more exciting films and performances, and educate even more responsibly and comprehensively. ... And if this goal remains too big and unattainable, people like to retreat into the shell of the private sphere."*

Not me. That seemingly unaffected people like to run away on the subject is understandable, but that does not make it any more acceptable. In addition, I have the experience that astonishing things are revealed once attention and memory are drawn to the topic. Providing a lot of material for a controversial but also constructive debate, which we urgently need to continue.

**Approaches**
At the beginning of this third part of the book I addressed how the professional-political examination of your métier can also strengthen you in dealing with your personal marketing. You could also say that with every bit you improve the (art) world in which you live (and are expected to promote yourself), you get closer to "Presenting without Pandering". So what can we do?

1. Self-image of the industry

    First of all, all artistic practitioners need to understand that they are part of the system—whether they like it or not. They are the industry. The third, anonymous woman quoted in the Zeit magazine (of January 4, 2018) on the case of the film and theatre director and artistic director Wedel aptly put it to me that an open door is a bad door to kick in. A bad reputation is a very good protection in these matters in the industry: "*The unanimous tenor of the press has been for about 40 years: ooh that Wedel, yes, a very bad one, especially with the women, downright obsessed, and on the set often a rager,* *but one of our greats, <u>the</u> director of German television. This image was supported by countless prominent colleagues who confirmed all this and in the end, however, were above all 'full of respect' and 'grateful' and had 'learned a lot' (and as I said: I probably would have confirmed this just as well if the collaboration had gone well and another colleague had been the focus)."*

Then artists, as part of this system, must be prepared to out their personal boundaries of good taste and, if necessary, to out themselves as spoilsports. All genders are called upon to express their displeasure when it becomes too shameless, too loud, too dirty, too value-free or too encroaching for them, so that no one can seriously claim: "*I always thought they wanted it that way,*" as several people—both in front of and behind the camera—revealed to me in the interviews. We must clearly call it out and say: Not me!

2. Prepare

    Information should already be provided in the training: Sexual attractiveness is a powerful currency in this profession. Others are: Skill, knowledge of the industry, your own abilities and limitations, a good network. You have to learn to deal with the fact that all beginnings are hard and that the feeling of not being good enough never quite goes away. That is part of the job—not the "casting couch". There are weapons to fight back with that can be both gentle and drastic. The best weapon, but also not all-powerful: a stable sense of self-worth. This can be built.

3. Transparency and contact points

    All professional artistic associations and institutions should set up contact points that can fall back on legal and psychological support. As co-author of the nationwide brochure on the "Risk Assessment of Mental Stress

for Artistic Employees in Theatres", I think: Why should there not be such a guideline for the industry, in which one formulates what is considered an accepted framework, what goes beyond it and which grey areas must or should remain?
4. Reduce pressure

   The existential pressure on creatives of all genres is and always has been high. On the one hand, it is necessary to improve our working conditions, whilst also reacting to the times in which we live, i.e. what are the pillars of my existence and identity besides art? Then on the other hand, to strive for behavioural prevention: how do I personally improve the way I deal with pressure?

Political scientist Ronny Patz, when asked how a media debate would lead to change, explained that the dynamics that lead to outrage are not the same as those that trigger change. For this to happen, he said, it would be helpful if there was already a parallel social process underway that the organizations concerned could take up. Moreover, there should be no one who has a blocking power against change. Whether an initiative like #metoo would have a chance of making such a difference? "*The increased attention can help, but only if the framework conditions are right.*" (Süddeutsche Zeitung, November 24, 2017, p. 11).

As a psychologist, I do not hope for the awakening of the "do-gooder". I prefer to trust in the human principle of orienting one's own actions according to personal benefit. In our world, a recognized place in the social fabric promises a high benefit. If we were to expect to be deprived of that place if we abused power or propped up an abusive system, we would certainly take that into account in our choice of means. At least, all of us who don't act on the basis of a mental disorder. And that is the vast majority.

So we know what to do.

# The Right Support: Coaches, Agents and More

At the beginning of the book, I compared the challenges for you as an artist with those in high-performance sport, pointing out that there a team provides for all the necessary skills. We then began by putting together your inner team of first, second and *Third Person*. Now we will look at what you would like to add to your inner trio and what you should pay attention to when expanding it.

Get into the *Third-Person* meta-level every time you seek support. Strategically and caringly align your choices with your private and creative persona:

- Get an impression in advance of the people involved, the institution, and what is being offered.
- Also include possible negative effects. It is very easy to affect people emotionally—especially creative personalities. However, to deal responsibly and competently with this fallout and to channel it in a meaningful way is much more difficult.
- Your *Third Person* should stand protectively in front of the first and second. Think carefully about who you want to let into your private and/or creative space.
- Once you have decided on something, stay alert to how the impact affects you and make a new decision if necessary.

You can't choose parents—but you can choose mentors, coaches and other guidance and support. Be aware of the high importance of the people by your side—both helpful and harmful.

**Coaching and Further Education**
At first glance, the range of further education, coaching and training on offer seems unmanageable. For artists, dealing with this always carries the risk of standing breathlessly in front of the supposedly huge gaps in their skills, repertoire and knowledge. Where are the priorities to be set? What would have the greatest effect on my progress? How much time should I commit? How much money? Take a look at your notes:

- How did you describe your personal habitat?
- What do you already know about the circumstances in which your second person can best flourish?
- What strategic goals has your *Third Person* defined for you?

If you choose on this basis, you will certainly already be able to filter what is available accordingly.

On the one hand, you are expected to independently ensure that you maintain your technical level and constantly develop yourself in parallel with the practice of your profession. On the other hand, workshops may sometimes seem to you to be the only way to feel alive. Temporary and even prolonged unemployment is part of the reality of life for most and gives many the feeling that they are no longer quite themselves.

> It is not always easy to distinguish between a sensible investment in training and an expensive illusion of work.

## The Right Support: Coaches, Agents and More

When it comes to further education, you should also be strategic and plan your interests and keep an eye on your resources—artistic, monetary and time.

- Do you know exactly why you are pursuing this advanced training?
- Do the techniques, styles and tools taught there improve your chances with regard to your long-term goals?
- And if not: is there another valid reason?
- For example, do you find it difficult to work alone?
- Would it be possible to form a training team of colleagues and to train each other free of charge?
- Does your educational institution have events for alumni?
- If not, what workshops and classes are on the market?
- Can you have a preliminary conversation or arrange a trial lesson or is there someone who can tell you more about it?
- Do you feel in good hands with the workshop leader? Are you seen, do you speak the same language, do you share the same attitude, or do you rather have the feeling that you, as a participant, have to prove the effectiveness of the method taught?

If you have unlimited resources, you can also use the "trial and error" method. Even then: avoid making sure of yourself through workshops. Again, if you have limited resources, don't cut corners. If further training is necessary to get closer to your goal, put yourself in competent hands, even if it comes at a price. Promotion and development of potential are a rare commodity. There are many working in this field—but not all of them perform what you would expect behind the blurb.

Paula, 34

> I studied acting at a university I won't name here, and there's one question that won't let me go: Why didn't anyone there ever recognize me for who I really am? I opened myself up so much, really put my heart and soul into it. In retrospect I realize: I was told a lot of nonsense about myself, which I also believed. It took me years to straighten that out for myself and realize my true potential. Does it have to be this way?

**Alina Gause:**
Your question is to be applied to all areas in which people are to be supported in their development—this concerns artistic leadership as well as parenthood and therapeutic offers. What kind of guidance makes people grow and what kind doesn't? We know from studies: the relationship is everything. The theory behind it, the ideology, the technique are secondary. So, your counterpart has to be capable of creating the right bond. What does that mean? He or she must be able to empathize with you. He or she must offer an appropriate degree of distance and closeness and must not be too needy in terms of attention. They should take an interest in you and invest time. Their view of humanity will also affect whether or not you are nurtured. Are you facing someone who would say with Viktor Frankl, "*To be human is always, always, to be able to become different.*" or rather someone who believes in one of the many type doctrines? And what about professional competence in addition to the ability to relate? Does the leader know his/her limits? If so— are they willing to have them exposed because your development is more important than their deficiencies? How much joy is there in seeing others shine? Recognizing a person and guiding them to their peak form is a complex task. Are educators in the arts prepared for this? No. Many of them succeed nevertheless. In the realm of higher education and artistic institutions, we depend on those in whose hands the unfolding of our potential lies to happen to have enough philanthropy, self-reflection, professional competence, and relational skills to do the job justice. So the answer to your question is: no, it doesn't necessarily have to be this way, but unfortunately it is very common and one of the biggest areas in the artistic profession where there is room

> for improvement. Students are in adolescence—a phase of life that is characterised, among other things, by the search for orientation. Therefore they intensively internalise what the instructors have to offer. If they do not have the aforementioned prerequisites for a successful working relationship, the damage is therefore all the more lasting, and so it takes some time to put things right. But take comfort: if you overcome these misconceptions about yourself, harmful attributions, superfluous stigmatizations, and professionally incorrect knowledge, you are guaranteed a high degree of self-knowledge and, in turn, a wonderful catalyst for the full development of your potential.

I often see creatives settling too quickly or being led astray by supposed miracle methods in their search for the appropriate accompaniment to their technical skills during their careers. This may be because they haven't yet enjoyed a fulfilling working relationship or are too impatient, or they don't trust themselves to distinguish good leadership from bad (see also under "Ouch Complex"). Just recently I experienced how a singer, who had intuitively taken good care of her voice for years, was vocally thrown out of balance by a few intensive lessons with a new vocal coach. This was due to the fact that she had been unemployed for a long period of time and was increasingly struggling with withdrawal symptoms from the lack of vocal challenges and was looking for new ones.

> Take care of yourself by carefully choosing and weighing the dose and source of training and education, workshops and techniques.

I want also to relieve you of making the pressure of the perfect choice: Every relationship—also every working relationship—means a risk. You trust, you show yourself, you expect, invest and hope. Without this openness, no bond can develop, but it can accordingly also be disappointing. Consider even unpleasant experiences as a useful source of information about each of your three personality parts, and continue to pursue your goal.

**Agencies, Management, Galleries …**
One of the most frequent questions I hear is about suitable representation such as agencies, management or galleries. Since access to these is still considered a quality criterion, it is usually at the top of the to-do list for artists. I agree that it can be a crucial help, but only under certain circumstances. If these circumstances are not right, an agency, management or gallery can even become damaging stumbling blocks in one's career. You wouldn't guess, for example, how often creatives are afraid to talk to their representation because the impression is conveyed that there is no time for them. That their concerns are misplaced or inappropriate. In the worst case, a conversation would always involve an evaluation of them or their art, which then accompanies them (too) long as a negative echo. This in turn affects their courage with regard to their own marketing activities.

I know of a particularly drastic example from the literary world. The author in question wrote a wonderful book that found immediate appeal with a respected literary agent. The agent offered the book on the market and here too it had resounding success: one of the biggest German publishing houses offered the author a contract and with it a gratifyingly high advance. The problem arose only after the signing: although the author had never given any hint in this direction, the agent had offered the novel as a biographical story. To this day, no one in the agency or at the publishing house knows exactly when who said what to whom for what reason, how and where. The author has suffered the damage—the book is on ice for the time being. It is to be hoped that it will still be made available to the public after it has been clarified. The great book would probably have found its publisher even without an agency—but that requires a lot of courage and stamina as far as (self-)marketing is concerned, because nowadays it is generally considered a no-go to offer a literary work without the mediation of an agency if you want to be taken seriously.

Another no-go concerns visual artists who are looking for a gallery. It is considered a faux pas when artists present themselves at a gallery without a recommendation or appointment. It's certainly legitimate for gallery owners to want to schedule, prepare and also pre-select. However to declare a law that says in which way gallery owners, gallery assistants and artists should find each other does not exist and that is a good thing. We are still in the culture business and not at an accountancy conference. As a rule, artists do not make use of an open gallery door anyway—their shyness prevents them from doing so. Once, however, in a workshop, I asked the participants which medium they would choose for establishing contact if they could choose it. I was very surprised when one visual artist said, *"I'd love to go unannounced to the galleries that suit me, with my paintings under my arm."* Everyone else in the workshop was as stunned as I was, because no one would have made that choice (and she remains the only one I know so far). I briefly enlightened her that she should expect resistance, and then we planned a showcase tour for her through German-speaking countries. I asked her to report back to me so that I could make the result available to other artists. She wrote to me that there had been some places where she had been clearly told that her taboo-breaking was not welcome. However there had been enough other examples where enriching contacts and conversations had taken place. One gallery had offered to exhibit her work. For her personally, though, the value of this trip would have consisted above all in the useful feedback and in the feeling that she had taken her own art *"out of the cellar and to the people"*.

> Deal with the confusing market of representations in your genre and form an opinion on what is the appropriate path for you personally.

An uneasy tension between creatives and their representatives can be fostered, among other things, by the fact that

- Too many artists are represented,
- No clear agreements were made (and set down in writing),
- Mutual expectations were not sufficiently clarified in advance,
- The lack of personal fit was underestimated in its impact due to other priorities,
- Both sides disagree about the strengths and weaknesses of the artist,
- Both sides define the product to be offered differently,
- Lack of competence and commitment on one of the sides,
- Monetary interests outweigh artistic ones (possibly for understandable reasons of not making enough profit to keep the agency or gallery going),
- Problems from other areas of life are transferred into this one.

You can prevent this through good research—both internally, in terms of your expectations, goals and preferences—and externally, in terms of what the market has to offer you.

## Checklist for Research and Preparation of an Application

### Research

- Research extensively what representatives and agents there are in your genre.
- Be prepared that this research can be psychologically very exhausting. Limit the daily time of the research to maximum 2 h and rather take up the thread again the next day (see also under "Office Time").
- Note whether your profile (type, style, age, subject, background) is already represented here and form an opinion about how that should be assessed. In the acting field, it is usually advantageous if your type is not already represented. In galleries, it may even be a requirement that you fit in stylistically well.
- Note positively and negatively remarkable things (design of the website, statements of the owners, profile, presentation of the artists).
- If you know someone in one of the agencies you are interested in, get in touch and ask about their previous experience.
- Note whether the website states which way people would like to be contacted.

### Application

- The best way is still personal recommendation. So if you have discovered names with which you have a positive or at least neutral relationship, check whether they could recommend you for an initial contact. Include indirect contacts for this, i.e. that you know someone who knows someone there.
- A cover letter should always show that you know exactly who you are applying to and why.
- Depending on the style of the addressee and your own personality, the application may be businesslike, chic, witty, personal or even unconventional.
- If none is specified, choose the medium that suits you best for your application: Phone, mail, postal, via social networks, in person? How do you prefer to communicate and what is most natural for you?

> - Make the access to your material as easy as possible: The addressees should be able to open everything with one click.
> - Name your links so that it is recognizable where they lead.

A good working relationship is built on mutual trust, respect and appreciation. This cannot be developed in one day. So it is quite common that a decision to sign a contract with a representation can drag on for a long time. So don't be afraid to keep your favourites informed of your progress if you have been signalled an interest in principle. Sometimes an important criterion for an admission is simply a matter of the right timing: for a certain window of time, the readiness for a new admission opens up. You want to use this moment for yourself.

The following case study is not only applicable to agencies, but also to all other professional representations in the field of art.

> Katherine, 33
>
> I'm dissatisfied with my agency. I wonder if there's any point in being in an agency at all. At the end of the day, the jobs come through myself for the most part. The fees are also no longer such that you want to give any of it away. But it's still considered a quality criterion whether you have an agency or not. What do you think?
>
> **Alina Gause:**
> Each agency can only represent a limited number of artists and the number of agency seekers far exceeds this. So you can say: Whoever is represented by an agency has been selected. Whether this has been to the advantage of one's career, however, remains to be seen, because as everywhere else, there are good and not so good agencies, and opinions differ as to what criteria should be used to judge this. The desire of art professionals to be selected sometimes weakens their judgement here. It either puts them in too passive

a position or raises their expectations of the agency into an unrealistic realm.

Let's approach the topic of agency search from an atypical but more profitable perspective for creatives: strategically. An agency provides a service that you pay for. Services are supposed to either relieve you or achieve what we can't do ourselves. In the case of agencies, both are sometimes a given and sometimes not. So it's not good per se to have an agency. When we delegate something, we no longer take care of it ourselves—that's the whole point. It's not uncommon for me to hear about agencies taking a cursory look at new photos, about callbacks that take days to return, or—as happened a few days ago—about an actor who refused to accept a lucrative offer and was put under a lot of pressure. Likewise, I hear from agents who deal intensively with their artists and help to develop and enforce steps together.

So it's not just about being selected and then letting things take their course, but being actively involved. Make yourself a list: What services do you even need? What can you do yourself? What can't you do, or what don't you have the time for? For example, research, providing opportunities to present yourself, and making contacts. Helping you make decisions regarding engagements and materials. Negotiating better terms and conditions. Guidance in career development. In overcoming career lows. Someone who believes in you. A scheduler. A go-to guy or gal. A shield to protect you. A reason to keep going. A figurehead, etc. Now rank these criteria in order of importance. What is most important? What does your agency support you in, and what does it not? How are others supported by their agencies in this? What runs on its own? In the end, there may not be that much left that you need an agency for—or do you? If so, ask for a conversation and now you can be specific about what you would like to see from your agency in the future. If there is little interest in this feedback on the other side, you can confidently go in search of another—with a clearer, more self-determined view of what.

Let yourself also be guided by your inner thread—the creative core—when choosing the right accompaniment and support!

## Family, Friends and Fans

Closely related to the "Ouch Complex" is the tendency of many creative personalities to devalue enthusiasm for one's own art when it comes from people whose connection is taken for granted: The circle of friends, partners and associates, family and fans. Family members and friends are not automatically fans. In fact, sometimes the opposite is true: they look at every move you make with particularly stubborn skepticism, or in the worst cases, contempt. In this case, they can become veritable authorities whom you spend a lifetime trying to convince that you deserve recognition. These cases are not what we are here to discuss, but rather about allies who faithfully believe in you when the rest of the world has yet to take notice. Of course, a professional will not be satisfied if the concerts are filled with grandparents and two fans. And if you haven't pulled off a masterstroke, motherly praise won't get you over it either. That said, I would caution against underestimating this resource. It's not uncommon for creatives to shamefully out themselves to me, "I'm only surviving this right now because my aunt is supporting me." "My brother does the website for me." "My husband has a good job—we put everything into my productions." "My girlfriend is my manager." As if that support is worth less because it's based on a bond. I encourage you to welcome any contribution to your progress.

> Artists deserve support.

Your artistic career is a business that needs several employees. Artists sometimes don't claim for themselves what is common in business: until a company is in the black, it often takes 3–5 years, during which the necessary input is preferably provided from within the company. The other day I heard the story of a very successful advertising agency. The three founders, who were also friends, designed the first years of their set-up by creating a shared flat that was transformed every morning into a respectable office where they could receive their clientele and present concepts. Beds were tucked away, the kitchen table was turned into a drafting table, chairs were set up, personal paraphernalia were hidden, carpets were rearranged, and decorations were changed. Then, after hours, the conversion back to an apartment was completed. There are many successful management and agency concepts that have their origin in a friendship or partnership. I don't need to mention at this point the well-known story of the painter Vincent van Gogh, who would probably have remained unknown to us without his brother. Appreciate and use this resource.

> Let your fans, family and friends comfort you, cheer you up, support you financially and morally and celebrate you.

Also take critical comments from these ranks seriously. People who are closely connected and well-disposed to you often have the best sense of when you are working past yourself. And also keep in mind: artistic careers do not run in a linear fashion, but in waves—those who have experienced another phase of great success after another know this very well. One actor described to me his awakening in this regard when, at an audition, he had to say his name and even spell it out at the reception desk for the first time in many years. True fans stay even when the business has just written you off.

# Excursus 2: Negotiations

Fee and contract negotiations call up all the difficulties creatives struggle with when marketing themselves. This is where the *Third Person* comes in and should be most attuned and prepared. That doesn't have to mean she takes it on herself. Their job may also be to realistically assess whether this task is better given to another person. Should the negotiating goblet pass you by as you are represented by an agency, management or gallery—very nice. However, even if you are not yet represented, you might want to look for backup for an upcoming negotiation, as some professional representations offer to take over individual negotiations without representing you long-term. I myself have handled it this way as an agent more often than you would think. This allows the artists to decide for themselves in which case a percentage fee seems appropriate to them and they don't have to pay any further commission if they don't want to take any service beyond that. Another concept that some resort to is to represent each other among colleagues. If necessary, someone who is otherwise unfamiliar with the profession can be helpful. I'm thinking of a young musician who I'm sure would have negotiated very well for herself, but was not taken seriously because of her youth. She worked on her offers, formulated the open questions and points to be negotiated, but then had an older friend communicate them.

> There is no universal recipe, but there is a bouquet of ways to make negotiations less troublesome and more effective.

Again, be deliberate and strategic:

> - What can I do?
> - What can't I do?
> - What do I want to learn?
> - What do I want to delegate?
> - How can I hand over financial, tax and contractual issues without losing track of my business situation?

Note that the answers to these questions may also change over the course of your life. Once again, as an artist, you are a one-person business. Take care of every department of your business, or make sure that they are working in your best interest. There are artists who have their business well in hand and others who tend to use the ostrich tactic and have a rude awakening when, for example, back or advance tax payments are due at the same time. Similarly when their contract doesn't cover sick leave or downtime due to bad weather. I've guided some in navigating their personal bureaucracy—what a sense of accomplishment! I want to encourage those of you who feel this is a good place to start: these things can be learned and mastered. Resort to the concept of "Office Time" to get started.

### Mareike, 26 and Betty, 28

> We both have a lot of trouble negotiating well for ourselves and wonder why that is: because we don't dare take money for something we enjoy, because we're women or because we don't think enough of ourselves? If we knew, we could do better in the future.

## Alina Gause:

First of all, we are good at everything we do with enthusiasm and interest, because we automatically demand from ourselves what it takes to become good at it. We search, collect and store information. We practice and seek out challenges to test our expertise in practice. Eventually, we gain expertise at it. Creatives can be passionate about many things—negotiation is not usually one of them. Just as we humans are drawn to something we are interested in, we avoid areas that bore or stress us and that we are confronted with being bad at. I assume this is the case for you with negotiations? The bad news is: it's not going to improve itself. The good news: it is possible that interest and enthusiasm for something that was originally unpleasant will grow out of dealing with it, and from that, in turn, competence. So if you really want to make a difference, this is where you need to start: approach the subject of negotiation, rather than just getting it over with quickly in an emergency. This is easier said than done—I'm aware of that. Negotiating for yourself as a "product" will call up all the uncomfortable issues you've already named: the industry's particularly tight market, the gender gap for you as women and the image of artists as supposed "self-indulgent navel gazers". Our meritocracy that has not yet understood that fun and self-realization are invaluable engines. Not only for performance but also as the best prevention against burnout, crises of meaning and a lack of work-life balance. So it is not surprising that you have difficulties negotiating well for yourself, because from the routine of daily justification towards your environment you classify your position as a negotiating partner as weak.

Look at it from the perspective of professional representatives who are not or less involved in these problems. How do they manage to negotiate well? They search for, collect and store information on what fees are currently being paid and do not allow themselves to be irritated by gaps in information because they know about the lack of transparency on the market. They ensure the best possible concentration through sufficient time and rest. They prepare themselves—calculate constellations and compare different scenarios of career developments. They bring in their respective personal qualities such as commitment, humour, decency, fighting spirit or charm, and they name the strengths of the product they offer for two reasons: they think it is suitable and they earn their living with it. So you see, there's no mystery behind good negotiation. Just work and personal commitment, and that's something you, as artists, are very familiar with.

**Checklist Contract Negotiations**

**Preparation**

1. Search, collect and store information
   (a) Which fees are currently paid for which performances?
   (b) What are the official and unofficial sources on this?
   (c) Are there any special costs involved in this engagement (travel, accommodation, cost of living in the region, training, material)?
   (d) Special tax features?
2. An own cost-benefit calculation
   (a) Fun/fulfillment, money, career advancement: which of these benefits is provided for?
   (b) Where are you currently in life and in your career? How should this be reflected in the contract?
   (c) What salary would subjectively make you feel appropriate and good?
3. Develop scenarios
   (a) Calculate different scenarios in advance and write them down so that you are prepared when it suddenly comes to: annual fee/weekly fee/monthly fee/lump sum?

(b) Consider how your desired fee can be achieved, if necessary, through tax-free supplements (housing costs, participation in agency commission or coaching).
4. The product
   (a) Make yourself aware of and, if necessary, note what service(s) you are providing.
   (b) Find words for your strengths so you don't have to look for them during the negotiation.
   (c) Don't forget why you are offering your product:
   - You think it's suitable.
   - Your counterpart also thinks it is suitable, otherwise they would not have made you an offer.
   - You do this for a living.

**Negotiation**

1. The Medium
   (a) If possible, choose your preferred medium—in person, by phone, by mail.
2. The circumstances
   (a) Ensure concentration through sufficient time and rest.
   (b) Have a notepad, pen, and your jotted down information and sample calculations ready.
3. Your style
   (a) Base your communication on your personal qualities and convictions, such as commitment, humour, decency, fighting spirit or charm.
   (b) Perhaps you want to deliberately differentiate the style of your *Third Person* conducting this negotiation from the style of the first and second person?

(c) Give yourself the chance to discover surprising new sides of yourself in this role.
4. The process
   (a) You may not complete negotiations at the first step.
   (b) Document each stage of the negotiations for yourself.
   (c) Take enough time: first listen to what your counterpart offers and get in touch after an agreed reflection period.
   (d) Obtain further information: are there statements made by your counterpart that you would like to check with colleagues or professional associations?
   (e) Repeat the preparation and then move on to the next phase.
   (f) Be aware that an ongoing negotiation demands time, mental and psychological capacity from you and plan accordingly.

# Presentation Material: Photos, Website, Social Networks Et al.

## Photos

Having portrait photos taken of yourself strikes at the heart of what most creative personalities dislike. This is because they want to showcase their skills, product or work and not themselves. This fact also surprises many who are not artistic themselves. Shouldn't artists—especially performing artists—jump in front of every camera that comes along? That is rather not the case. Not all of them, of course, but a great many artists regard the production of portrait photos as a chore that they only perform when they absolutely have to. In doing so, they underestimate the necessity, postpone the task again and again or don't tackle it at all. If a photo is then unexpectedly requested—for the cover of a book, an application, social networks, PR, the programme booklet or to illustrate an interview—they have to fall back on material that the second person does not adequately present. In the acting field, this part is usually well taken care of: the subjects renew their photos at least every 2 years. In the field of literature, graphic design, music, musicals, directing, dramaturgy, scriptwriting—even photography—it is not a given to have a photo at hand with which one presents oneself willingly and well. Your *Third Person* should know that it is much easier to advertise with a nice photo and make sure that one is available in the future.

> Take the production of your photos in hand and design them—like everything else—to your taste. Then you will be able to achieve very good results and, if necessary, even spend a nice day.

First of all, it is important to know what the photos are needed for. Portraits for acting probably need to meet most of the specifications: the gaze should be directed primarily at the camera. They should mainly depict the basic personality of the performer and deliberately deviate from it in some additional motifs (with glasses or headgear, possibly historical or scenic-looking). A full body photo and a close-up should be included. Creatives in the field of music, visual arts, authors and writers usually only need one or two press photos, which they can use for years. You are completely free to do what you see fit. Your portrait may or may not reflect the expression of your art. If you feel like countering that—be my guest! In music and musicals, there is more freedom in how you present yourself than people often think. As a result, we see a lot of photos where the sitters seem interchangeable to us. I would encourage you to let the creative core set the tone here as well. Potential employers are visually inundated. The quality of photographs has improved enormously in recent years—achieving a well-lit, hand-crafted image is not as difficult today as it was 20 years ago. All the more our viewing habit is geared towards optimally coiffed, made-up and exposed people, and we skim over the many good-looking people looking back at us. An individual expression therefore evokes the most interest. There is an acting coaching institute that has wallpapered its lobby with portraits of all the actors who have taken classes there. I'm always amazed when I'm there at how quickly my eyes get used to it and I judge very good photos as uninteresting and don't really notice them. I'm amazed that this photo wall place in particular keeps pointing out this frustrating fact. Think carefully about what is important to you in your photo. What do you want to communicate? For these thoughts, put yourself back in the (meta-)position of the *Third Person* who wants to present the second in the best possible way. The private person has a break at this point and the creative one has to surrender trustfully.

| Checklist photos | |
|---|---|
| **What matters** | **What doesn't matter** |
| Minimum technical standard | Top technical performance |
| Sufficient time | A lot of time |
| An idea from the photographer, how he/she can realize your needs | That the photographer puts his/her artistic vision before your needs |
| A relaxed and dignified atmosphere (who can support you on location if necessary?) | A design of the session adapted to the needs of the photographer. A good photographer knows that he/she will take a better photo of a model who is relaxed |
| Photo sessions are exhausting - be prepared to have a hard day's work of you (which can still be enjoyable) | A top brand photographer |
| Good preparation (outfits, sleep, water, makeup, hair) | That the photographer likes you |
| Clarity from all involved as to what the photo is meant to communicate. This requires good preparation - expecially if photographer and artist did not know each other beforehand | That you work with the makeup artist that the photographer recommends<br><br>That you are a model |

## Website

Having your own website is definitely helpful. It gives you the opportunity to shape the perception of your overall personality in a self-determined way in one place on the net. It's not uncommon for artists who don't have their own website to have the Wikipedia or Google entry take over this function, which is unfortunate. When I started this paragraph, I initially thought "Readers will think I think they are elementary school students!" However just when I offered free telephone consultations in spring 2020 during the Corona crisis and wanted to find out in advance in a nutshell who I was about to speak to, I was only able to do so in half of the cases and then also learned in the conversation that one's own homepage has already been eking out its existence on the to-do list for ages.

Today, creating a homepage is easier than ever. You yourself determine the degrees of freedom of the design depending on your own competence. You can say: The freer the more difficult. A clear, modular concept without frills is enough for you? You can do that yourself. You want it complicated? Then seek professional support.

It should also be mentioned that a website is not absolutely necessary. Perhaps you work in an institution that presents you very well on the net? There is no law according to which you are only professionally positioned with your own website. For performers who work exclusively in the film industry, having their own website may even miss the (marketing) mark. They should be represented on all casting platforms with the professional entry. It is much more important than having your own homepage to keep your profiles up to date and to present special skills such as languages or sports with small videos. If a casting agency gets lost on its own website, where possibly the category "News" is not filled appealingly, experimental theatre improvisations or other side paths of the creative personality are presented, it might not lose interest, but the overview and therefore the interest. Accordingly, a homepage of one's own is important for all those for whom the net does not offer a tailored presentation opportunity. Especially visual artists have to face the challenge to adapt the presentation of their art to this medium. I am thinking here, for example, of an artist whose works of art are hung like pictures but have a three-dimensional texture. Photographs do not transmit the appeal of these works. She found the appropriate presentation in a special video format. Videos of installations are often as unappealing as videos of stage productions. It is worthwhile to activate the second person here and to find your own art form for the presentation. This also applies to singers, for example, when it comes to vocal demos. Of course, a professional can tell if a live recording is impressively clean. However there are many clients who, when listening to a demo, still follow our general listening habits and thus expect (because technically processed) perfect intonation.

> The website is not the expression of your personality—that is your art. The website is the communication tool to present this art as well as possible.

In order to determine for yourself whether a website is necessary and if so, what you should present there and in what way, start with a first simple step: search yourself on the net.

> **Search Engine Test**
>
> Enter your name in different search engines. Does the result correspond to what you would like to convey about yourself to potential work partners?
>
> Draw conclusions from this test as to whether there is a need for change, and if so, where:
>
> 1. Are your products to be found?
>    It should be possible to get to one of your works with two clicks. Click 1: your name. Click 2: to the picture, the

video, the link, the platform, the website, where one can directly enjoy your singing, playing, painting or other artistic expression.

2. Are you presented in sufficient quality?

    Here the following applies: Do not show anything on the net that does not do you justice—less is more! You want to arouse curiosity, not saturate the need already at this point.

3. Is your bandwidth sufficiently mapped?

    This is true for those of you whose product is primarily versatility. Think carefully about what you want to include in your offer.

4. What is the likelihood of confusion with the competition?

    In workshops, this often results in interesting suggestions for discussing an artist's name or pseudonym. For example, one artist with whom I conducted the test discovered that she had a very successful namesake. Since the competitor was far ahead of her in name recognition, she decided to make a slight name change. Others report that they can't be found because their name is so difficult to spell (at least in German-speaking countries) that there are always typos.

5. Compare the result with your findings from reading this book so far: does the picture correspond to where you want to go in the long term and what you identify with?

    Maybe everything is as it should be and yet you do not like it? Maybe you have already developed inwardly and outwardly this is not reflected well? Once a participant in a workshop told me that she could no longer listen to her self-introduction (which had just been highly praised by the others). She's been reeling it off unchanged for years because she always gets good feedback for it, but she's increasingly uninvolved in it. Then think about how you might change that. How would you like to supplement or thin out the material?

6. Whenever you create material, also consider how sustainably it can be used.

    An introductory video may not be relevant after only 6 months because your hair looks different, you may or may not be pregnant, and the list of your credentials has changed. A musical demo recording, on the other hand, may remain interesting for a lifetime. Include these considerations when estimating how much to invest.

At the risk of tiring you with repetition, I would also like to remind you of the policy of small steps when it comes to websites: Approach the target state office time by office time. Sometimes you manage very quickly the right little clip for the self-introduction, the good text, the appealing portfolio, sometimes it takes months until you can bring together all the ingredients or even have a bright idea.

> **Guide to Planning a Website**
> 1. Research
>    (a) What is common in your subject?
>    (b) Do you agree with this or would you like it done differently?
>    - (Then do it differently!)
>    (c) What already exists?
>    (d) What do you like/dislike about it?
>    - To do this, create files with the examples that you can show to a web designer to explain yourself, if necessary.
> 2. Benefit
>    (a) What benefit would you like to get from the website yourself?
>    (b) Who do you want to use your website?
>    (c) For what?
>    (d) What are the consequences (e.g. languages, webshop, calendar)?
>    (e) How long term should the website be designed?
> 3. Preliminary work
>    (a) Create a draft based on what you already know. Choose your preferred material for this: paper, Word file, cards, mind map on a flip chart, …
>    (b) Gather photos, videos, texts, press releases, audio samples and similar promotional material that you expect to use in one file.
>    (c) Note any open questions.
>    (d) Get into conversation about it—with people whose assessment you find helpful. What do they think about your material, the benefits, your target audience?

4. Creation
   (a) If you want to create the homepage on your own: research the current providers for this, look at the templates, the prices and the handling. There are countless advantages to taking it into your own hands. Tackling it alone doesn't have to mean tackling it all by yourself. Take the first steps and draw on others' experience when hurdles present themselves. At the beginning of the book, I went over the psychological importance of "self-efficacy." Especially if creating a website doesn't come easily to you, this process will add significantly to your self-efficacy account.
   (b) If you would like to entrust the creation of the homepage to other hands: take your time in finding the right partner for this, in terms of costs, agreement on aesthetic issues, reliability of communication and commitment to completion.

Finally, some bad news and some good news. The bad: creating a website is usually tedious and time-consuming. The good: with this work you do a lot of what you have to do anyway in terms of profile raising, material creation and self-promotion.

## Social Networks

Social media is a fast-moving medium. My children, for example, would consider it completely superfluous to deal with Facebook in more detail today. Therefore, I don't want to go into the use of the specific social networks, but rather suggest how you can basically approach such a tool, which has the sole purpose of self-marketing and may be privately repugnant to you. I choose Instagram as an example because it is currently the most common cause for despair in consultations.

Some people just have it in them. They have a knack for presenting themselves visually. They like to do it often, feel in their element there and accordingly have many followers. To those, I certainly have no added value to contribute. On the other hand, I would rather address those who are not at all comfortable with social networks. This (large) group can be split again: on one side are those who don't care. They let social media be social media and are welcome to keep it that way. On the other side are those who personally dislike it, but assume a professional gain for themselves in it and therefore want to face it. This part is meant for you.

I've touched more often on how disastrous it can be for creative personalities to feel disconnected from what they're doing. So the goal is to not approach Instagram in the way you experience it when you look in, i.e. alien, ingratiating, inconsistent with your own values. Rather make it your own. Social media is a tool—a means to an end. You need to subdue them. To do that, I recommend the following:

Guide to Creating a Profile in the Social Networks

**Step 1:**
- Don't expect to enjoy dealing with it. This is hard work!

**Step 2:**
- Familiarize yourself with it. Look into it. Get upset about what you find terrible. Take a longer look at what you like. Take note of what makes the difference.

**Step 3:**
- Be aware of who you would like to be perceived by with your public self. And also who you think you are perceived by. Is there an "ideal fan"? Instagram is designed to send this ideal-fan information about you because they're excited about it, not to annoy them. So give this model addressee an age, a gender, a face, a worldview, maybe even a name? As an aside, this ideal fan can be consulted on all marketing matters and imagine how he or she would judge your activity.

**Step 4:**
- Develop your own Instagram profile without already creating it publicly. Design different posts—texts, announce-

ments, photos, little movies. Maybe you have ideas for regular promotions (raffles, work samples, announcements)? Anything you can't stand behind 100% will be discarded. Besides your own opinion, check again and again whether your ideal fan would like the post.

### Intermediate step: Technology check

Have you noticed when drafting posts that your posts don't have the same visual, audio and design quality as others?

- Check the special settings of the respective platform.
- Check your know-how in handling camera, microphone and image composition.
- Check your technical equipment. Even for little money, amazing improvements can be achieved today.
- Ask savvy friends. If you like web tutorials, you will find answers to these questions on the Internet.

### Step 5:

- Create an archive for these posts so you're never embarrassed to fall below your quality standards when you haven't posted anything in a while and are tempted to post something that doesn't suit you just so something of yours can be seen.

### Step 6:

- Create an Instagram profile that is solely for your professional needs. Instagram is a Third-Person communication channel—the private person has no place here. Unless you want to deliberately mix that boundary for strategic reasons and share pictures of your family, kids, hometown experiences, your wedding or private dinner there. Otherwise, use an incognito profile for this and for cat videos.

### Step 7:

- Post.

**Et al.**

With the following exercises, we want to once again specifically train your *Third Person* as the main actor in the matter of your self-marketing. There are many situations in which she has to promote you abruptly. Imagine again the situation I mentioned when introducing the *Third Person*: you are sitting in a small circle at a private birthday party. You assume that you are sitting here exclusively as a private person. Completely unexpectedly, the person sitting next to you turns out to be an employer who is professionally attractive to you, and you inevitably make the switch from private to *Third Person*. Maybe you are called in the supermarket in a professional matter that is crucial for you or you accompany someone to a premiere and suddenly the press officer wants to interview or photograph you. In these moments, whether you like it or not, you switch to the *Third Person*. It's more comfortable if you're prepared for it, and that preparation should be able to develop over a period of time. This increases the likelihood that it will be an authentic second skin and not a put-on shell.

The *Third Person* takes over the communication for your product. That is, it must represent it as well as possible in attitude, language, appearance, effect, image. Not in the sense of a likeness, but rather in the sense of a management that you would also want, when representing you, to show itself in a way that you agree with. Your *Third Person*, where they show themselves, should convey to those around them that the artist in you

- Loves what he/she does,
- Brings willingness to perform and ability,
- Takes responsibility,
- Is cooperative where he/she is met cooperatively,
- Has a sense of humor,

- Is attentive to his/her environment and
- Is not willing to do anything at any price.

> Preparation of the *Third Person*
>
> - To equip your *Third Person* well for self-promotion challenges, prepare now, even before you are surprised by a situation:
> - Literally make a picture of your *Third Person*
>   - What outfits might suit her for different scenarios?
>   - In what do you feel comfortable and free and not dressed up and inhibited?
>   - Let media and people inspire you on how you would like yourself best.
>   - If styling isn't your thing: maybe you'd like to get some support for that?
> - Carry your information material with you
>   - By no means should you impose your business cards or flyers on others in an inappropriate manner, but should you encounter someone who wants your contact information or material about you, you should have it ready and not be in need of scribbling your phone number or next presentation date on a receipt.
> - Practice talking about yourself
>   - Share with your friends and family, with your partner, what you find difficult about this. Perhaps they can give you useful suggestions for describing yourself and your art?
>   - In the "Elevator Pitch" exercise below, I offer a procedure for you to practice presenting yourself alone or in pairs.

> **Exercise "Elevator Pitch"**
>
> The term "Elevator Pitch" comes from the idea that you meet a professionally interesting person in the elevator and you want to manage to present yourself within the short ride in such a way that a further contact develops from it.
>
> The aim of the exercise presented here is for you to understand what you personally need in order to feel comfortable in the role of the self-imaginer. The more comfortable you

feel in it, the more comfortable your counterpart will feel with you. Beyond that, it's also about figuring out what information you want to use to best introduce yourself according to your request.

**Solo version**
(a) Try telling a fictional person in 60 s who you are, what you do, and why you are worth working with or purchasing your art.
(b) If you don't succeed as you would like, try a first step of spending 60 s advertising for a colleague you admire. Please speak in the first person singular ("I am...") in this version of the exercise.
(c) Finally, make a note for yourself (if necessary, also in writing in bullet points):
   - What do you feel comfortable or uncomfortable with?
   - How can you determine this—mimic, gesture, language, content?
   - Which information do you consider important in the future, and which should be neglected?
(d) If you initially introduced yourself as someone else: If necessary, repeat the self-introduction again from your own perspective.

**Duo version**
You can also arrange to do this with a real-life counterpart.

(a) First present yourself in front of each other.
(b) Share how you felt and what you noticed.
(c) Then for the partner presentation, agree on what should be included in the presentation from the point of view of the person presenting. Presenters should also actively ask questions in order to feel well placed to present the other person in the best possible way.
(d) Then present your counterpart. In this version of the exercise, too, please speak in the first person singular ("I am...").
(e) Finally, record together (if necessary also in writing in bullet points):
   - What differences did you notice between your own presentation and that of others—in terms of content, atmosphere, facial expressions and gestures?

- Which parts of which version would you like to keep in the future?

(f) If necessary, you can also present yourself again in conclusion and check whether you can already tell that you feel more confident and comfortable with it.

4. Actively give permission to the outside world to look at you.
   - One of the reasons Third-Person situations are so unpleasant is that it feels as if one is powerlessly at the mercy of the other person's will. This is because they are usually evaluative situations where supply clearly exceeds demand. Actively remind yourself that this is a temporary state that you have chosen for yourself, because this is the condition for getting to your destination. Speak silently to yourself, "It's okay. You may look at me. I give you permission to do so."

### Group Exercise "Exhibition"

The following exercise illustrates the impact that being consciously looked at already has on us. It enables you to try out how you can transform the feeling of powerlessness into a feeling of self-determination if you express an inner permission to do so.

This is a silent exercise.

1. Divide the group.
2. One half is spread out individually in the room—as if they were exhibits in a gallery.
3. The other half takes on the role of the exhibition visitors for about 3 min. They go from exhibit to exhibit, looking at one more extensively than the other, from the front, from behind, depending on taste and mood. The "works of art" can be looked at.
4. Then visitor-half and exhibit-half exchange roles.
5. Join the conversation afterwards:
   (a) How do the roles differ?
   (b) What surprised you?
   (c) What was unpleasant and why?
6. Repeat the exercise with silent but inwardly active permission to the environment to look at you.
7. Share your thoughts: Have you noticed a difference?

We have reached the end of the third part. Perhaps you have already done the exercises and taken action to accompany the reading, or this path is now before you. Either would make me happy. Ultimately, self-marketing for creative personalities means nothing less than finding and creating their place in life.

> You are not faced here with the decision of whether or not to advertise yourself, but rather the choice of the place you want to assign to your creative activity in your life.

To retreat from self-marketing would be to retreat from life. Once you have really faced this "monster" and got to know it, there are many advantages: the perception and appreciation of your art through better visibility is only one. Another is that you will be able to better understand what is going on in the market, which in turn will allow you to act more efficiently. Furthermore, addressing self-marketing will not be a lifelong unfinished business. If one day you decide to pull your creative substance from the marketplace to let it flourish in a protected place, that will then be a self-determined decision. Looking back won't hurt if the path looked different than you initially imagined.

Many artists still let themselves be dictated to about how success is to be defined. In doing so, they overlook the potential they have to create a fulfilling and vibrant life for themselves. There are many roads to Rome—in terms of self-marketing and in terms of success. There's the soap star who writes da-da poems and performs them in his hometown. The cellist who tours the world 3 months a year and spends the other 9 caring for his four children. The director who, at the age of 50, has made her second feature-length film but earns her living in other ways. There's the guitarist whose only CD, the one he spent 10 years working on, went straight to CD of the Year (by the niche jazz community). Heartily adored by his fans and fellow musicians, he nevertheless lives in circumstances that might generally be described as precarious. In turn, can't screenwriters make it their goal to earn money from their profession rather than make arthouse films or their own projects? Can artists decide for themselves? They can. All of them. You too. It's your life, your art, your self-marketing.

# In Conclusion

Nelson Mandela, in his inaugural presidential address, used a quote from Marianne Williamson (from "A return to love") to remind us humans that we should put our strengths at the service of humanity. It is not our darkness, she said, that scares us most, but our light. By shining ourselves, we give others permission to do the same. If we ourselves were liberated from fear, others could feel liberated by our presence.

You are an artist. Your strength is to always feel, want, seek and give a little more. Unfortunately, creative personalities often fear that they are "too much". Too loud, too deep, too emotional. Too serious, open, playful, naive, critical, demanding. Too passionate, dreamy, needy, sharing, sensitive, vulnerable. Too wild, too ambitious, too complicated, too colorful, too curious.

For many, therefore, the only places where they feel appropriate and adequate are the stage, the studio, the film set, the workshop or the orchestra pit. There, they don't worry that there's anything wrong with showing themselves free, radiant, and at their fullest. Feel free to give to the world what only you can give. In this sense, understand self-marketing as your duty to at least offer your contribution to the world. Show yourself.

# References

Brown, Brene (2017). *Verletzlichkeit macht stark*. München: Wilhelm Goldmann Verlag.

Belafonte, Harry https://www.zitate.eu/autor/harry-belafonte-zitate/91620 Zugegriffen:18. April 2020

Campbell, Joseph (1994). *Die Kraft der Mythen. Bilder der Seele im Leben des Menschen*. Zürich: Artemis & Winkler.

Campbell, Joseph (2011). *Der Heros in tausend Gestalten*. Berlin: Insel-Verlag.

Gause, Alina (2011). *Warum Künstler die glücklicheren Menschen sein könnten. Der Künstlerberuf aus psychologischer Perspektive*. Norderstedt: BoD.

Gause, Alina (2016). *Kompass für Künstler. Ein persönlicher Wegbegleiter für Kreative*. Berlin: Springer Verlag.

George, Götz (2020). https://goetz-george-stiftung.de/stiftung/motivation/ Zugegriffen: 18. April 2020

Harris, Russ (2013). *Wer vor dem Schmerz flieht, wird von ihm eingeholt: Unterstützung in schwierigen Zeiten. ACT in der Praxis*. München: Kösel-Verlag.

Harris, Russ (2009). *Wer dem Glück hinterherrennt, läuft daran vorbei: Ein Umdenkbuch*. München: Kösel.

Hüther, Gerald (2020). https://kulturwandel.org/inspiration/interviews-und-texte/wie-gehirngerechte-fuhrung-funktioniert/Zugegriffen:18. April 2020

Marks, Stephan (2016a). *Scham – die tabuisierte Emotion*. Patmos-Verlag.

Marks, Stephan (2016b). Arbeitsmaterial Seminar *"Menschenwürde und Scham – Die Bedeutung von Würde, Scham und*

*Scham-Abwehr für die psychosoziale Beratung"* vom 11. bis 13. April 2016 in Freiburg.

Shaw, George Bernard (1984). *Mensch und Übermensch.*

Maslow, Abraham. (1943). *A theory of human motivation. Psychological Review, 50(4), 370–396.*

Reis, Jack (1997). *Ambiguitätstoleranz.* Roland Asanger Verlag.

Tarr Krüger, Irmtraud (1993) *Lampenfieber. Ursachen, Wirkung, Therapie.* Stuttgart: Kreuz Verlag.

Thurnhofer, Hubert (2014). *Die Kunstmarktformel.* Norderstedt: BoD.

Vogler, Christopher (1998). *Die Odyssee des Drehbuchschreibers.* 2., aktualisierte und erweiterte Auflage. Frankfurt am Main: Zweitausendeins.

Williamson, Marianne (2016). *Rückkehr zur Liebe. Harmonie, Lebenssinn und Glück durch "Ein Kurs in Wundern".* München: Goldmann Verlag.

Printed by Printforce, United Kingdom